C000263164

Graham Tomlin is Bishop of K. much of his life teaching theolo quite a few other books, loves m order), and spends far too much

'I kept saying "YES!" as I turned the pages of this book. Again and again, Graham Tomlin puts his finger on things I've struggled with both personally and professionally. He has a rare ability to make confusing things clear and complex things simple. *Why Being Yourself Is a Bad Idea* pulls no punches. It gets right to the root of the Western psychosis, offering an ancient, time-tested, more hopeful alternative that rings deeply true.'
Pete Greig, 24-7 Prayer International, author of *How to Pray*

'Most books about religion are boring. This one isn't. It is intriguing and provocative, speaking to our deepest concerns and heaviest questions. In beautiful prose, and with a wide range of reference, Graham Tomlin unpacks a whole world . . . and it is a spacious and attractive one. This exposition of faith in the twenty-first century arrives at a simplicity the far side of complexity. The book is a real gift.'
James Mumford, author of *Vexed: Ethics beyond political tribes*

'This book presents Christianity in a fresh way for the times.'
Winston Marshall, Mumford & Sons

WHY BEING YOURSELF IS A BAD IDEA

IS A BAD IDEA

And other countercultural notions

Graham Tomlin

First published in Great Britain in 2020

Society for Promoting Christian Knowledge
36 Causton Street
London SW1P 4ST
www.spck.org.uk

British Library Cataloguing-in-Publication Data
A catalogue record for this book is available from the British Library

ISBN 978-0-281-08179-0
eBook ISBN 978-0-281-08180-6

1 3 5 7 9 10 8 6 4 2

Typeset by Fakenham Prepress Solutions, Fakenham, Norfolk NR21 8NL
First printed in Great Britain by Jellyfish Print Solutions

eBook by Fakenham Prepress Solutions, Fakenham, Norfolk NR21 8NL

Produced on paper from sustainable forests

Contents

A bit about me and this book

Not many people get to do the job of a chess piece. But I do. I am a bishop. I didn't particularly want to be one. It's not the kind of work you apply for – you just get asked to do it. My job is to look after churches – large ones and small ones, across a stretch of west London in the UK. Church is, to be honest, a mixed bag. Sometimes it can inspire you with the most spine-tingling sense of the presence of God or incredible acts of devotion and self-sacrifice. Sometimes it makes you cringe as Christians fight over tiny scraps on Twitter like ferrets in a sack. When I wonder why I do this job, I keep being reminded that I do it because I think these small communities of people, often forgotten and sometimes feeling a bit sidelined in the modern world, actually contain within them the mystery at the heart of the universe, the secret of living and dying truly, a secret I began to discover for real when I was a teenager and have been exploring ever since. It's not that I don't have my doubts – of course I do, like any honest Christian. But in my clearest and best moments, this way of understanding the world and living life makes more sense to me than anything else.

Two thousand years ago, a revolution began in a small backwater of the Roman Empire. It barely registered in the histories of the time. An awkward, provocative Jewish rabbi caused a minor stir in Roman *Palestina* and was swiftly and successfully silenced not long after he started going public. Yet, within fewer than three hundred years, the Emperor himself was a follower of this executed teacher and the revolution that the latter started began to infiltrate cultures all over the world. In the following centuries, it inspired some of the most magnificent buildings the human race has ever produced, shaped the imagination of some of the greatest artists, poets and philosophers, and framed the lives of countless people across the planet, marking their vital moments of birth, marriage and death, guiding them through disasters and delights, politics and pandemics.

Today, Christianity is the world's largest faith, with 2.3 billion people – almost 30 per cent of the world's population – claiming to be followers of Jesus. But the numbers alone are not the reason I believe, and it's not why I think you should either.

C. S. Lewis, the author of the Narnia stories, once said, 'I believe in Christianity as I believe that the sun has risen: not only because I see it, but because by it I see everything else.' If Christianity makes sense, it does so not just on its own terms, but because it makes sense of everything else. It offers answers to some of our deepest questions. Of course, today we are much more technologically advanced and scientifically knowledgeable than people of the past. However, we still look into a dark night sky and marvel at our smallness in a vast universe just as they did; we still cry agonizing tears when we lose our friends and family or when a relationship breaks up, just as they did; we too ask questions about the meaning of life, freedom, suffering, just as they did. The science may have changed, but human nature does not change that much. The questions we ask are remarkably similar to the ones that our ancestors struggled with in the past.

The Christian revolution is one that changes the way you look at the world; the way you feel about yourself. It always seems strange to begin with, which is why many people don't give it a second look, because it contradicts so much of what we think of as common sense. Another part of my job – and this bit is more than simply a job, it's something that I think about all the time – is not just to understand this for myself but also to try to help other people understand it. This book, if it's to make a half-decent fist of explaining Christianity, has to question a number of things that seem obvious to us these days. The chapter titles are deliberately a bit provocative, because what it offers is a kind of countercultural wisdom to many of the things we take for granted in our world, things that, if we carry on living this way, will destroy us and this precious planet that is our home.

No book is ever a lone effort. I'm grateful to friends who helped to shape it through conversations or reading it before it came out and so helped to make it better than it would otherwise have been. I'm grateful, among others, to Tim May, Rupesh Patel, James Mumford, Lydia Corbett, Peter Jones, Jonny Bayfield, Pete Wynter, Al Gordon, Winston Marshall, Graham Charkham, Marcus Mumford, Sian Brookes and Sam Tomlin. Thanks too to all at SPCK – to Alison Barr and Michelle Clark – and to my copy editor Nick Fawcett. Not all of them will agree with everything in the book, but they have helped me to do a better job of trying to show how Christianity, despite everything, offers a way of life that is much richer, fuller, more disturbing, costly, yet utterly worth living – a life where we learn how to live together in a world that we did not make.

Trying it out might be the best thing you ever did.

1
Why 'being yourself' is a bad idea

Have you noticed how we talk about ourselves these days? Phrases like this trip off the tongue: discover yourself, indulge yourself, express yourself, be kind to yourself, look after yourself, be yourself. The 'well-being' or 'spirituality' section of any local bookshop will have titles like *Learning to Love Yourself, Believe in Yourself, Know Yourself,* or *Respect Yourself*.

There is an online clothing brand that calls itself 'Be Yourself'. On its website is a poem that captures exactly what many people believe about themselves these days:

> Let them judge you,
> Let them misunderstand you.
> Let them gossip about you.
> Their opinions aren't your problem,
> You stay kind, committed to love,
> And free in your authenticity.
> No matter what they do or say
> Don't you dare doubt your worth
> Or the beauty of your truth.
> Just keep on shining like you do.
> BE YOURSELF

It's a classic statement of modern life. Don't listen to negative voices, just be authentically yourself. If we had ten commandments in the modern world, it would be number one.

We are a culture that has become obsessed with the self. Wanting to boost their self-esteem, we tell our children that they are special, they are amazing, that there is nothing they cannot do if they put their mind to it, that the world is their oyster.

Yet, with all this focus on the self, it hasn't seemed to make us much happier. In 2019, Gallup produced its regular 'Global Emotions Report', and the headline ran: 'the world is sadder, angrier, and more scared than ever before'. The 'Negative Experience Index' remained at a record high, yet the countries that scored lowest on negative emotions (in other words, those less likely to feel bad about themselves) were places such as Azerbaijan, Latvia, Poland, Mongolia – not generally the western European or North American ones that are particularly focused on the importance of self-regard. The most positive countries were in South America – again, not the ones we'd expect.

You would have thought that Western countries with a strong ethic of personal fulfilment and economic wealth would be the happiest, yet according to the 'Happy Planet Index' – a survey that 'tells us how well nations are doing at achieving long, happy, sustainable lives' – the USA is 108th and Sweden (for example) is 61st out of 140 countries surveyed.[1]

Some psychologists suggest that this focus on self-esteem, indulging, expressing or simply being ourselves has only served to breed a generation of self-absorbed, troubled souls. Using a test for narcissistic traits in American college students, researchers discovered that evidence of self-regarding behaviour has rocketed since the 1990s, and the consequences are grim:

Narcissism causes almost all of the things that Americans hoped that self-esteem would prevent, including aggression, materialism, lack of caring for others and shallow values. In trying to build a society that celebrates high self-esteem, self-expression and 'loving yourself', Americans have inadvertently created more narcissists.[2]

The self turned inwards

Martin Luther – the German monk who kicked off the Reformation, that great shift in European cultural life which led to the split between Catholics and Protestants in the sixteenth century – had a striking way of describing the human condition: 'our nature has been deeply curved in upon itself'.[3] It is a vivid picture of the self turned away from other people and into self-absorption and worry.

Do you ever find yourself worried about what others think of you? Whether you have made the right choices in life? Anxious about how many followers, likes or retweets you get? Why other people seem to live so much more interesting or successful lives? Maybe those thoughts occupy a lot of your waking (and dreaming) time and when they rear their heads, chase any other more positive thoughts out of your mind?

How do we explain this inner curvature of the self? There are basically two ways of looking at it. One approach says that it basically comes from greed. We want to grab what we can from life and fear that others might get there first, so we become competitive. We cut ourselves off from others because they are rivals in the race for limited resources – whether money, fame, promotion or sexual conquest.

The other explanation is more sympathetic. Our most painful experiences in life, most of which we can hardly remember – the time when we were abandoned by a parent, laughed at by those we thought were our friends, rejected by someone we loved deeply – those experiences left a deep hurt somewhere inside. Out of fear of being hurt again, we defend ourselves by shrinking into ourselves, sometimes even physically, resolving never to be that vulnerable in future. We view the world with suspicion, expecting it to hurt us again,

'Cynicism is usually the hard crust of a hurting soul.'

so we guard our own selves jealously. Cynicism is usually the hard crust of a hurting soul. We become self-absorbed, defended, repelling all boarders, not trusting anyone. We can hide it well, continuing with an affable exterior, even apparently having lots of friends, yet inside, we closely guard our hearts by turning in on ourselves and away from the dangers of a hostile world.

A culture turned inwards

The deeper problem is not just that we do this as individuals, but that we have done it as an entire culture over the past few centuries.

Will Storr's book, *Selfie: How the West became self-obsessed*, tells the story of the love affair between Western societies and the self.[4] It describes the various ways in which the self has been understood in past societies, but focuses on the extraordinary growth of self-focused therapy and ideology in more recent times. Storr visits California, the home of self-expression. It was here, he says, the idea took root that our true inner selves were god-like, needing simply to be liberated from the constraints of social convention and moral repression. He examines the neo-liberal ideas of Ayn Rand (1905–1982, the novelist–philosopher and author of *The Fountainhead* and *Atlas Shrugged*) that lay behind the economic policy of liberalization – the notion that the individual entrepreneur needs to be liberated from regulation and constraint in order to be free to take part in the competitive marketplace of a capitalist society. He takes in Silicon Valley, the home of the digital revolution, and describes the internet as the epicentre of self-promotion – a flat structure where no one is in control, where everyone is free to express an opinion and promote him- or herself. His most telling observation? When we developed the technology to take pictures anywhere and anytime with devices we carry with us everywhere, what do we mostly take pictures of? Ourselves.

'When we developed the technology to take pictures anywhere and anytime with devices we carry with us everywhere, what do we mostly take pictures of? Ourselves.'

Charles Taylor is a Canadian philosopher who has put his finger on the way we think about ourselves in the modern world and how that's different from the way people thought in the past.[5] At one time, most people believed that they fitted into a large cosmic order, held together by God or some kind of universal moral law (some religions, like Christianity, Judaism or Islam, tend towards the former; others, such as Confucianism, Taoism or Buddhism, to the latter). The point about this wider structure was that we didn't choose it; it was just given. To find wisdom or moral guidance, therefore, you looked outside yourself, to God or the moral law, to give that guidance.

Over the past couple of hundred years or so (although the roots go back further than this), many people in the West have abandoned faith in God or any sense of a given cosmic order. As a result, there is no longer any overarching 'sacred structure' that holds the world together, so we are left on our own as individuals in it, without any predetermined order that tells us who we are and gives us a sense of security and 'fit' within a wider scheme of things. Of course, we actually find it impossible to live in total chaos, without any structure whatsoever, so we have to manufacture it ourselves.

Where, then, do we look to find moral guidance and direction? We look inside. We look not to the heavens or the hills, but into our own hearts. No longer embedded in a wider cosmic order, we are driven back on ourselves. With no map for the journey, we have to make up our own. We stop looking outside ourselves to God, the stars or the wisdom of the past, and start to look into our own inner emotions and desires. Taylor calls it the 'subjective turn' in modern culture.[6] It's not that people didn't think about themselves at all in the past, but they tended, in pre-modern times, to look into their

> **'Where, then, do we look to find moral guidance and direction? We look inside. We look not to the heavens or the hills, but into our own hearts.'**

own hearts to find hints of the moral or spiritual laws that held the universe together (as Plato did) or to find traces of the divine nature (as St Augustine did in his masterpiece of early autobiography, the *Confessions*).

In the eighteenth century, the idea began to grow that each of us has our own particular way of being human, our own individuality that trumps everything else. And so, to find moral direction, we search our own inner selves to find our true identity, assuming that our true selves are hidden somewhere within our hearts, and the clues to that identity are found in our strongest and loudest desires and longings.

The overriding moral law therefore becomes to be true to that self. We get the cult of authenticity, where the only true imperative is to be authentic, to 'be yourself'. Remember the poem?

> . . . free in your authenticity.
> No matter what they do or say
> Don't you dare doubt your worth . . .
> BE YOURSELF

Left and right – but much the same

This, of course, is played out in our politics. Everyone says these days that we live in a more polarized world. Contrasting visions – left and right, progressive and conservative – compete for political and social power, whether in the USA, Europe or in parts of Asia and Africa.

The vision of the right makes a priority of individual choice, allowing market forces to take their course, assuming that a free market will eventually bring prosperity for all. Loosening restrictions on the market and the entrepreneurial activity on which it depends will enable a thousand flowers to bloom and lead to a flourishing economy for everyone. And bearing in mind the imperative to acquire the goods needed to live a successful life, our role in this is to act primarily as consumers, buying the things we need to live that life and keep the economy going in the meantime.

Now there is truth in this. In general, many people have been lifted out of poverty across the world in the last hundred years, which is a great gain for the human race. However, it isn't all good news. In 2008, the global economic crash, sparked by rash lending of large sums to Americans who wanted to buy houses they couldn't afford, revealed how unstable that kind of economy is and how it doesn't really end up creating a fair playing field for all. The poorest were the ones who lost their jobs and livelihoods as a result. The coronavirus pandemic of 2020 also revealed the same pattern: that those who lived in more cramped housing or did jobs that couldn't be transferred to home working were more likely to suffer than the better-off and more 'professional' classes. On top of that, we have become increasingly aware of the effect that this kind of consumerist economy has on our planet. The search for cheap packaging and transport for goods, and the desire to maximize the financial return on land use, has led to oceans clogged with plastic and forests decimated across the world.

The vision of the left, on the other hand, sees not the market but the state as the key agent. The market cannot be trusted, as it will always end up with inequality and is inherently unstable, so the state has to step in to dictate and control our economic and social behaviour. Traditional left-wing politics prioritized social justice, championing the cause of the poor, those left behind in the race for economic wealth and social success.

Again, there is value in this. The welfare state in the UK, with the NHS and the vision of state-provided free basic healthcare for all, is one that is almost universally loved on this side of the Atlantic. The wider difficulty, however, is that it is hard to find examples of left-wing states that have not ended in the economic difficulties and, hence, widespread poverty of North Korea or Venezuela, or the stifling conformity and control of Soviet Russia or the former GDR. More recent versions of left-wing activism champion not just the economically poor but also an identity politics that widens the range of those deserving equality and liberation to a whole host of other marginalized groups, defined by ethnicity, gender, sexual orientation or numerous other self-identified characteristics.

Both sides are locked in the well-known culture wars, but what is often not recognized is that, underneath, they want the same thing. They are both focused on a view of human beings as rights-bearing individuals, free to fashion their own version of the good life. Both see the goal of their political programme as liberation of the individual from the shackles of either state control or social taboos, to be and do what they choose. Both assume that we are all essentially individuals in need of liberating from other people who make demands on us, so that we will be free to chart our own self-chosen path through the world.[7]

Rights or wrongs?

Alongside this, we had the rise of the idea of human rights. It was assumed throughout the classical and medieval periods that free-born men (and just men) had certain rights they could claim from wider society, but at some point in the early eighteenth century, those rights began to be ascribed to all people, regardless of gender and wealth. The UN Declaration of Human Rights was published in 1948 after the Second World War. From then until the 1960s, the idea of human rights worked to defend the individual against repressive governments that might deny free choice in a number of vital areas of life. They were needed to ensure that governments could not randomly execute people, imprison them or confiscate their property.[8]

In more recent times, human rights have in effect become the predominant way – in fact, perhaps the only way – in which we can speak about morality. Within the framework of 'rights' language, the individual could claim rights over and against the claims of government, family or social expectations, strengthening the position of the individual self as supreme over all things. The problem is that it is notoriously difficult to establish who has the responsibility to ensure or deliver on those 'rights', and how you decide what is a valid right and what isn't. If someone asserts a right, does that establish it? If I assert a right to breathe clean air or access free public transport, who can tell whether that is a right or not, and who is responsible for delivering it? Rights language, however useful in its proper place, can easily become the fence we build around our sense of self, our autonomy and independence. The result of this combination of the cult of authenticity, the imperative of self-determination and the language of rights, is that no one has the right to question another person's choices. Or if they do, the inevitable response comes back: 'Who gives you the right to tell me what to do?'

The result of all this is a bewildering range of ideals and as many goals for life as there are people. There is little sense of any common idea of what the good life is. You're meant to find that out for yourself. What you choose to have as your goal in life is a personal decision and no one can tell you otherwise. That doesn't mean, of course, that there is no common ground

'There is little sense of any common idea of what the good life is. You're meant to find that out for yourself.'

at all – it's just that the common ground is all about the means, not the end. German sociologist Hartmut Rosa suggests that there is no agreement in the modern world on what it means to live a good life, so we are left with a kind of ethical pluralism as the norm. Yet he points out that we do have almost universal agreement on the preconditions needed to get to our version of the good life. To attain a good and happy life, in whatever shape you want it to be, you need to secure enough money, friends, knowledge, health and rights to achieve it: 'Secure the resources you might need for living your dream whatever that might be. That is the overriding rational imperative of modernity.'[9]

The secret to a successful life is to get better skills and knowledge to land the dream job that will enable you to make a difference in the world, while at the same time giving you enough money to buy what you need to live that life. It requires being healthy enough to enjoy sport or just be pain-free and attractive enough to draw admiring looks wherever you go and find your ideal life partner. You need influential friends who can advance your cause and help to bend the world in the direction you want it to go. You need the confidence to stand up for your rights – what you deserve. We are all in a race to acquire these keys to a good and happy life, even if what that life looks like is entirely self-determined.

Problems in the cult of self

But does this work? What is the usual advice given to every young person going for a job interview, a first date or an important meeting? 'Be yourself.' It's hard to think of more confusing advice. The one thing most of us are afraid of

'It's hard to think of more confusing advice.'

above all is that people will actually see our inner selves, will hear the thoughts that lurk inside our heads, the things we think but are mighty glad no one else can see. Much of what we find on social media is people trying not to present their real self, with its doubts, anxieties and failures, but a carefully crafted sanitized version that will win everyone else's approval, measured in likes or retweets.

'Much of what we find on social media is people trying not to present their real self'

The people who genuinely say the first thing that comes to mind are usually the ones who end up in trouble. Thinking only of 'being yourself' makes you turn all your attention on yourself, which is the last thing you should be thinking of if you really want to be of use to, or even to attract, other people. When you think of the people who are good to be with, who make you feel alive, who help you to be a better person, they are usually those who aren't thinking about themselves much at all – they are far more interested in you.

'When you think of the people who are good to be with, who make you feel alive, who help you to be a better person, they are usually those who aren't thinking about themselves much at all – they are far more interested in you.'

Then again, who is this 'me'? Half the time I don't know what I think about all kinds of issues in the world: one day I feel good about myself, the next a bit down about life or a bit ashamed of myself; my likes and preferences change from week to week, let alone from year to year. Trying to grasp and identify this elusive essence of who I am often feels like trying to grab water with my fist.

If being true to yourself is the only moral imperative, if being authentically 'you' is the only law you have to obey (providing, of course, that you don't harm others – more of that in Chapter 8), then each one of us has the responsibility to chart our own future. In doing that, the source of wisdom we have to consult to help us is not God or some idea of Goodness, but ourselves. Individual choice becomes paramount, but the difficulty then is that there is no way to adjudicate objectively on the value of those choices. Take two people, for example. One has decided that, to be true to herself, she needs to live a life travelling the world, flying from place to place, getting all the experiences she can, being independent of anyone else, doing odd jobs every now and again to fund her nomadic lifestyle. The other person decides that to be true to himself, he needs to become a nurse, devoting himself to the sick and those worse off than he is. Which one is more valuable? If the value of a course of action is found solely in the fact that someone has decided it is the path that is most true to him- or herself, how on earth do we adjudicate between the values of different paths? This is where it gets difficult and contradictory.

What we really need are what Charles Taylor calls 'horizons of significance' – a sense of what really does matter and what doesn't, and some way of adjudicating between them, to give some weight to certain choices over others. Otherwise, living a lifestyle that attempts to save the planet is inherently no more valid than deliberately acting to ruin it.

Now, we instinctively don't think this is right. It can't be right to trash the planet. So we do have to set limits on self-expression, but then it becomes difficult to do so, if we have already established the primacy of the self and its freedom to be what it chooses to be, and the right to it.

The poem we started with has at its heart an unresolved tension. It says:

> You stay kind, committed to love,
> And free in your authenticity.

'You can either be "free in your authenticity", ignore what everyone else says, be true to yourself and forget the rest, or you can be "committed to love", to listen to others, to focus on their needs and perspectives rather than your own.'

It sounds good, but you can't have it both ways. You can either be 'free in your authenticity', ignore what everyone else says, be true to yourself and forget the rest, *or* you can be 'committed to love', to listen to others, to focus on their needs and perspectives rather than your own. That dilemma gets right to the heart of the problem of the modern sense of self.

We are a culture that has 'turned in on itself'. The habits and hurts that shape our individual lives are also played out in wider culture. The more damning explanation, again, is greed. As early modern Europe devolved into nation states, all competing for the riches of other parts of the world that they colonized, they turned against each other and fought wars for power and empire, often using religious differences as a front for economic ambition. The other explanation, again, is more sympathetic. Burned by the experience of what were sometimes called 'religious' wars (and religion was certainly implicated in them, even if they weren't the only or even the predominant factor), western Europeans turned away from God and any sense of a wider moral structure to the world, and were left alone to find their own way. In the meantime, levels of loneliness and anxiety rise, our politics has become increasingly polarized and our way of life is destroying the planet on which we live: 'the world is sadder, angrier, and more scared than ever before'.

But what if there is another way? What if the visions of left and right, conservative and progressive, aren't the only ways to live? What if competitive, consumerist individualism, the cult of self, is a dead end?

What if the way to find our true selves, paradoxically, is to let go of them first? What if you find yourself not by looking within, but by looking outside yourself? One modern translation of one of Jesus' sayings runs like this: 'Self-help is no help at all. Self-sacrifice is the way, my way, to saving yourself, your true self. What good would it do to get everything you want and lose you, the real you?'[10]

What if we find our true selves not by looking within but by being drawn out of ourselves by something outside? In the spring, as the sun begins to warm the air and the earth, you begin to see barren land sprout flowers and bare branches are soon covered with leaves. The warmth of the sun brings out the hidden potential lying deep in the sap of the trees or the seeds planted deep in the soil. A tree in summer has become its true, glorious self (if we can put it like this) not by regenerating itself from within but by being drawn out by the sun as it sheds its light and heat. Maybe we too become our true selves by turning not inwards but outwards, towards a source of life that is constant, steady, waiting for us to turn in its direction?

But that raises the big question: is there really anything beyond us or are we alone in the universe?

2

Why wonder is the beginning of wisdom

Are we alone in the world, all trying to find our true selves, without any wider framework or wisdom to guide us? Or is there something – maybe even someone – out there that gives us a common purpose, a direction that we didn't choose, yet that actually points us towards true happiness, even if it doesn't always look like it at the time?

Let's start with the question of whether there might be a something or someone out there to give us a sense of direction. It all begins with a universal human experience: Wonder. In other words, being willing to say that we don't know the answers and allowing ourselves to be simply amazed at what comes our way.

When I left school, I did the gap year thing, travelling to the Indian subcontinent to see the world with a few friends. Roaming around the foothills of Nepal, we decided not to use one of the local hotels, but instead to head into the woods to sleep. We collected sticks, made a fire and huddled in our sleeping bags as a cloudy day came to an end and night fell. I couldn't tell whether it was the cold or the dawn that woke me. As the first glimmers of early morning light appeared, I was dimly aware that the fire had gone out and the cold was beginning to make me shiver. When I opened my eyes, what I saw made me forget how cold I felt or, in fact, anything other than the sight that lay before me.

Looking into the distance, where the night before had simply offered a grey, overcast sky, suddenly now there was a vast range of snowy peaks, slowly turning yellow and then orange as the sun lit them. It was the first time that I had seen the Himalayas and they were so much higher, bigger and whiter than I had ever imagined. The sight was literally breathtaking. I woke my friends with a whisper – speaking loudly seemed somehow sacrilegious in front of such beauty – and we sat there, awestruck, not speaking a word for around half an hour, while the sun rose, lighting up the mountains with a constantly changing palette of colour.

It was a classic experience of wonder, yet it was more than just a spectacular view. I have often thought about that moment as, like many other such moments (I guess we have all experienced something vaguely similar), it seemed to me to offer a way into understanding something about life and its meaning. I now think that such experiences are a kind of clue to the deepest questions we puzzle over occasionally.

At the time, I remember one of my friends remarking how such an extraordinary vision confirmed her belief in God, as surely something so beautiful could not have come about by accident. I'm not so sure. The argument from design – that an intricate world necessarily requires a creator – doesn't really work as a slam-dunk argument for God. There are other ways to explain how an intricate and beautiful world emerged from very modest beginnings. The theory of natural selection makes a decent fist of showing how complex organisms can evolve from quite simple ones, as a result of the necessity to adapt to survive. Arguments for God from the incredible design of the universe may have some merit, but they're certainly not knock-down arguments and can't bear much weight. In fact, most Christians think it is impossible to prove the existence of God, however good the arguments that religious people stack up, and for very good reasons – reasons that will become apparent later in this chapter. No, the reason that I think such experiences give us a clue to transcendent reality rests not on some argument from design, but on another approach altogether.

Toast and travel

The two most famous Greek thinkers, Plato and Aristotle, both believed that wonder was the beginning of all philosophy. Awe is a universal human experience.

We are all stopped in our tracks once in a while, amazed at a glowing sunset, the birth of a child or

'Awe is a universal human experience.'

an extraordinary act of kindness that causes us suddenly to forget ourselves in fascination at what we have just seen. To wonder at something is to recognize that it might not have been like this; in fact, it might not have been at all. Seeing that stunning early morning view was remarkable because it was unexpected. I simply did not know that something as spectacular as that was possible – which is why it was so impressive. When my wife gave birth to our first child, the sense of wonder and joy I felt was bound up with the recognition that it might have been otherwise – we might not have been able to have children; our son could have died in childbirth, as many newborn babies have done in the past, or he might have been a different child. The particularity of his existence, his character, his face being what it was, rather than any other, was a source of amazement and surprise, a sense that only grew larger as he did.

What, then, do you do with such an experience? The problem is that we tend to absorb knowledge of this new thing into our view of the world, so that next time we see it, it doesn't seem so remarkable and it fails to evoke wonder any more. If I had lived in that Himalayan clearing, waking up to that view every morning, I'm sure, in time, it would have become a bit predictable, something not quite so remarkable as it seemed that day, precisely because it was expected. And this is what can happen to any of us. As we grow older and more experienced in life, we can get to the stage where nothing is remarkable, nothing arouses a sense of wonder, because we've seen it all before.

In one of his short stories, Julian Barnes imagines someone dying and going to a place that sounds a bit like heaven.[1] In this place, every wish is fulfilled, every dream comes true. Eventually, his football team wins the FA Cup every year, he gets so good at golf that he is able to go around every course with eighteen holes-in-one; he has met all the famous people who ever lived and has had sex with all the beautiful women he can think of. The trouble is that, having done everything, everything becomes boring. Eventually, he chooses to go into oblivion because nothing else can satisfy – there is nothing more to surprise, nothing more to do.

One way to try to get over this sense that things eventually get dull and routine is to go on a never-ending search for new thrills, new places, the adrenaline rush of endless excitement. The last fifty years, at least before the coronavirus pandemic stopped us in our tracks for a while, has seen an explosion of world travel as a result of greater personal wealth and cheaper flights, coupled with a greater knowledge of other cultures due to the world-shrinking power of the internet. These days we are more eager to have experiences than to own things. We want to be continually surprised and need to find new encounters to amaze us. The problem comes when the money runs out or even when (if it were possible) we've literally seen everything there is to see. What then?

'These days we are more eager to have experiences than to own things. We want to be continually surprised and need to find new encounters to amaze us.'

The opposite of wonder is familiarity: that normal dull way of perceiving the reality confronting us every day, which we simply assume is going to be there whenever we look at it. My regular piece of toast for breakfast or the cup of coffee that goes with it do not normally evoke much wonder, given that I have seen them countless times before. In fact, to get to the stage where nothing seems remarkable, where nothing evokes any sense of awe, is to reach a stage of life that is profoundly troubling. It is a poverty of spirit that is not too far removed from depression, a sense of the weariness and predictability of everything.

This was an experience that the Romantic poet William Wordsworth knew well. One of his most famous poems begins like this:[2]

> There was a time when meadow, grove, and stream,
> The earth, and every common sight,
> To me did seem
> Apparelled in celestial light,
> The glory and the freshness of a dream.
> It is not now as it hath been of yore;—
> Turn wheresoe'er I may,
> By night or day,
> The things which I have seen I now can see no more.

Like many a jaded adult, he recalls the sense of wonder he had as a child with sadness that it has been replaced by dreary familiarity. The 'glory and freshness' have faded away and the world no longer has the aura of wonder that it once had. Later in the poem, Wordsworth foresees the day when his own child will be weighed down with the routine nature of things:

> Full soon thy Soul shall have her earthly freight,
> And custom lie upon thee with a weight,
> Heavy as frost, and deep almost as life!

This experience of a world that seems dull and familiar, where everything is customary, predictable and unexciting, is something that troubled many of the Romantic poets, not just Wordsworth.

To arrive at this point sucks all the joy out of life and leads to a world-weary cynicism. When 'been there, done that' becomes the response to everything, you've reached a dull and dangerous place.

Yet, towards the end of the poem, Wordsworth envisages a condition in which the least experience can bring back that sense of wonder at even the most ordinary of things:

> To me the meanest flower that blows can give
> Thoughts that do often lie too deep for tears.

He knew that a child-like capacity for wonder, at 'meadow, grove and stream' – in fact, 'every common sight' – is infinitely more valuable than the adult world-weariness that can no longer wonder at anything.

Small children, of course, have an infinite capacity for wonder because, for them, everything is new, experienced for the first time. Everything is amazing, even if they aren't quite sure yet whether new things are pleasurable or terrifying. As we grow older, habit tends to replace awe, we get used to things and life becomes comfortably predictable, except for those brief moments when the sheer beauty of the world breaks in on us, as it did for me on that morning in the mountains.

The experience of wonder can lead us in one of two directions. Either it takes us on a trajectory of finding ever-more amazing encounters until every box has been ticked, every thrill known, so that there is nothing left to wonder at, or every moment of delight or awe alerts us to the remarkable fact that things exist at all.

If you walked down a street later today and saw a miniature rainbow hovering in the air above the the pavement, you would be astonished. You might ask what it is and how on earth it came to be there. Yet, in reality, it would be no more amazing than anything else existing – the people walking past, the shops around you, the sky above your head or the pavement beneath your feet. You might also ask the same questions of them: what exactly are they and how did they come to be here?

Our occasional experiences of wonder can lead us to marvel at the very miracle of existence – the remarkable fact that there is something rather than nothing. In this way of thinking, the distinction between the vision of mountains and the piece of toast or the cup of coffee begins to dissolve. The slice of toast might be familiar, but in one sense it is no less miraculous and a potential source of surprise than a newborn baby, a spectacular view or an inexplicable rainbow above a pavement.

Life itself is both mysterious and fragile. To have lost a loved one is to recognize how tenuous is our hold on existence. To realize that a spouse or parent or child is no longer there is to recognize the fragility of life. At the same time, the thought that those we love and who remain alive around us might one day not be there usually increases a sense of gratitude, and even wonder, that they are there at all.

Most people would agree that this capacity to be delighted at the very miracle of being, even of the most ordinary things, is a much better way to live than the jaded, world-weary cynicism that is incapable of being surprised at anything, or even the constant, never-satisfied search for new experiences and thrills. Of course, you can't live in a state of amazement always – you have to get on with life and that means accepting its predictability. But

'this capacity to be delighted at the very miracle of being is a much better way to live than the jaded, world-weary cynicism that is incapable of being surprised at anything'

being able, every now and again, to stop in your tracks and marvel at the sheer wonder of a flower, a friend, a conversation, a stone or a piece of art is part of what it means to live a good, healthy and enjoyable life.

What might (not) have been

To wonder at something is to recognize the essential mystery of things. It might not have been this way. It might not have been at all. To use a philosophical term, it is to recognize the contingency, rather than the necessity, of the world. Necessary things just have to be – they could not have been otherwise. Contingent things are dependent on something else and might have been otherwise.

Yet it is the next step that is the most interesting one. If existence is contingent – in other words, this world is not necessary; it did not have to exist, and nor do I, and nor do you – then it naturally leads to the question of how it, or we, came to exist or why we exist at all.

It is possible to answer those questions by looking at the physical causes of the phenomena that strike us as remarkable. You could explain my surprise at the vision of the mountains through an explanation of the weather conditions in north India on that particular morning, the refraction of light and my inexperience of Himalayan topography. You could explain the birth of a child through the biological processes that brought her father and mother together and the intricate interplay of sperm, eggs and chromosomes that determined her emergence into the world in that particular form. You can account for a piece of toast by a description of the wheat that was ground into flour that was turned into bread, the electronics of the toaster and so on. In each case, you can trace the event back through ever-regressive layers of dependency to some kind of original starting point. In other words, you can answer the question of why something exists by a huge chain of cause and effect, a massive game of Chinese whispers, back to the original first cause.

A number of books have appeared recently, by physicists and others, claiming that they can show how the universe has arisen spontaneously from nothing, without the help of God or any transcendent cause. They offer a range of theoretical models as to how the universe emerged from one form of existence to another; for instance, the idea that the laws of nature themselves are sufficient to explain the origins of the universe or that the tiniest particles – so miniscule that, to most of us, they appear non-existent – could have given rise to much more complex forms of life. To take one example, Lawrence Krauss's book, *A Universe from Nothing: Why there is something rather than nothing*, claims to be able to explain why the universe exists without recourse to anything transcendent, such as the idea of God.[3] The difficulty is that when he gets round to explaining what he means by 'nothing', it isn't really 'nothing' at all. It is what he calls 'empty space', which, of course, is not really empty at all, but contains all kinds of electromagnetic fields, particles, force fields and so on. He might or might not be able to demonstrate that this 'empty space' could generate more complex entities and ultimately life itself – I'm not a scientist and don't consider myself capable of knowing whether he has shown this or not – but I do know that he hasn't demonstrated how something can come out of nothing, only that something can come from something else. He hasn't been able to show how this empty space, with its electromagnetic waves, virtual particles, fields and forces, came to be in the first place.

All of these arguments seem to me to make a simple category mistake. Laws might describe how something exists, but they don't make it exist. The laws of rugby describe how the game works; they don't invent the game in the first place or cause it to be played. Similarly, purely material expla-

'Laws might describe how something exists, but they don't make it exist.'

nations for the emergence of the universe only ever explain how something actually comes from something else. They don't explain, and neither could they ever explain, how something emerges from absolutely nothing at all. You can argue back to some small, infinitesimally tiny element of matter, which seems as good as nothing, and then show how the world might have emerged from it, but that doesn't get over the vast, yawning gap between nothing and something. 'As good as nothing' is not nothing and never can be. The difference between the complex forms of life that we know now and the microscopic particles or electromagnetic forces from which they may have emerged may be vast, but we can imagine how the former might develop from the latter. What is impossible to conceive is how those microscopic particles or electromagnetic forces can have appeared from – literally – nothing at all.

'All this would seem to suggest one thing: the universe does not explain itself.'

All this would seem to suggest one thing: *the universe does not explain itself.* The experience of wonder points to the radical contingency of everything we see, feel and touch. It points to a world that might not have been. But if it might not have been, why, then, does it exist at all? The bottom line is that an explanation of this conundrum cannot be found within the world itself. Everything that is contingent is dependent on something else.

The biggest fish of all?

The key point is this: not everything can be contingent. If everything is dependent on something else, every step leading to another, at some point the staircase has to stop. There has to be some ultimate place where it rests – some final, ultimate cause – that doesn't need any further explanation.

At this point, the dispute between religious and non-religious people often takes a predictable course. The religious person might see this argument as one that points to God as the first cause of all that exists. Someone had to start the whole thing off, and when you trace the long process of cause and effect back to the beginning of time, you find yourself with the finger of God, triggering the Big Bang, as it were, by (to use another image) pushing the first domino that causes all the other dominoes to fall. God is invoked as the missing piece of the jigsaw, the one who explains the gaps that science can't explain, such as what or who lies at the mysterious beginnings of the universe.

The atheist, however, would reply with something like this: 'OK – you say that God is the explanation for why there is something rather than nothing, but believing in a God doesn't solve the problem, it just takes it one stage further back and leaves you with the difficulty of explaining the origin of God himself. Who made God? Who created the Creator?'[4]

The trouble with these arguments – the religious and the non-religious one – is that they both make the same category mistake. They both think of God as another object within the universe – granted, a very large and influential one – but one that explains mysteries, fills gaps, makes things happen. If this is true, then, because he exists as another thing within the universe, he requires some kind of explanation as to why he exists in the first place, like everything else in that universe.

This is where a bit of conceptual clarity may help, identifying what Christians and, for that matter, most monotheistic religions mean when they use the word 'God'. They certainly don't mean a very large, complex and dominating person or object existing somewhere in the universe or even alongside it;

> **'By definition, when they speak about God, Christians are referring to something, or someone, uncreated, the one entity that is not made by anything else, but just is.'**

the one who flicked the switch to turn the lights on in the first place. By definition, when they speak about God, Christians are referring to something, or someone, *un*created, the one entity that is not made by anything else, but just is. If everything we see around us is *contingent*, God is the only being that is *necessary*. God is not dependent on anything else, but is the one on whom everything else depends. God is not something within the finite universe, or any universe, but is the infinite wellspring of all being, the source of all that exists. When we speak of God, we're not referring to the finger that pushed the first domino, but the reason all the dominoes exist in the first place. He is not the cosmic Architect working with stuff already made – he is the Creator who made the stuff from nothing. God is not the craftsman who made the world, in the same way as the carpenter made the table or the engineer the car – he is the reason why carpenters, tables, engineers and cars exist at all, and continue to exist. The difference between God and everything else is not a question of relative size, power, age or even origin, but of ontology, of being itself – God is a different kind of being altogether.

'God is a different kind of being altogether.'

Christians (and others) use two terms to describe God; they say that he is transcendent and immanent. Transcendent means that he is beyond and outside the world, not just within it. Immanent means that he is, at the same time, always present to it. This means that God is not just the creator but also the sustainer of all that exists. Not only did he start it off but also it depends on him for its continued existence at every moment.

That is why God's existence can never be proved. We sometimes look for evidence of God's existence. There are pointers, indications, of course – miracles, prayers that seem to be answered and the like – although, admittedly, it is always hard to prove they are not coincidences. You can prove or disprove events, ideas or theories because each of them relates to and is connected to other things within the universe, so you can tell whether they make sense or not or whether there is enough historical or observational evidence to amount to reasonable proof. What Christians mean by 'God', however, is by definition beyond all that exists within that system and, therefore, not subject to our normal types of proof. In fact, most religious traditions, at least monotheistic ones – those that believe there is only one God – suggest that God is beyond human comprehension in any case (unless, that is, God were to choose to make himself known in terms that we could understand – more of that later).

The question 'does God exist?' is, in fact, not as straightforward as you might think. To most people it seems just like asking the question 'does Mount Everest exist?' or 'does the tooth fairy exist?', to which the obvious answer to the first is yes and to the second is no. Both Mount Everest and the tooth fairy are entities that either exist or don't exist within the universe, and the question of whether they exist or not can be decided by bringing forth evidence, or the lack of it, within a network of observation, deduction and causality. When we talk about God, however, we're talking about something else altogether – namely, the reason why anything exists at all. We are asking whether the universe really does explain itself or requires an utterly different source that is, by definition, uncreated and uncaused, transcendent and immanent outside the physical world, not contained within it. We are talking about the one necessary source that explains the existence of all contingent reality. As David Bentley Hart points out: 'it makes perfect sense to ask what illuminates an object, but none to ask what illuminates light. It makes perfect sense to wonder why a contingent being exists, but none to wonder why Absolute Being "exists".'[5]

There is a description of God in the Bible that says this: 'In him we live and move and have our being.'[6] This gets it right – God is not another fish in the sea, the biggest fish in the sea or even the original primeval fish from which all other fish derive; he is the sea in which all fish swim, in which they live and move and have their being. That is why arguments about the existence of God are often like fish arguing about the existence of water or, to use another image, a bit like characters in a novel arguing about whether the author of the novel exists or not.

How many gods do you believe in?

The other objection that pops up regularly is along these lines: 'You believe in one God, right? In other words, you're not a polytheist and you don't believe in the many gods of paganism or Hindu mythology? Well, like you, I don't believe in them either, it's just that I also delete one more god – yours.'

This argument makes exactly the same mistake as the previous one. It assumes that what Christians mean by 'God' is what polytheists mean by 'gods'; the former believe in one, the latter believe in many – it's just a matter of how many gods you happen to believe in. But, again, this is a simple category mistake. Polytheistic religions, those that believe there are many gods, such as ancient Greek paganism or Hinduism, do, of course, believe in many gods, but most have also held to the distinction between the one transcendent divine principle behind all the other gods and the various, so-called 'divine' beings that wander in and out of the universe. Deities in the various types of Hinduism are often viewed as emanations of an underlying principle called Brahman, which represents the many facets of ultimate reality. It's not exactly the same as classic monotheism, but it does indicate a distinction between the many gods and the essential reality of which they are a manifestation. Sikhs conceive of the one God who is the maker of Brahma, Vishnu and Shiva. Ancient paganism, in the times in which Jesus lived and the earliest churches emerged, believed in many Greek gods – Apollo, Bacchus, Aphrodite and the rest – but would often at the same time distinguish between them and the one divine principle that stood behind them all, particularly in more Platonic modes of thought.

In other words, the 'gods' of polytheism are a kind of higher form of nature – a bit like the angels or demons that turn up in the Bible and other forms of Jewish or Christian literature. Christians have never believed angels were divine – they were just supernatural beings, in the sense that they were super-natural – above ordinary nature, but still part of the wider order of created things (at the risk of repeating myself, this is not to try to argue at this stage that angels, demons or pagan 'gods' do or don't exist – it's just to try to clarify what we mean by the terms we are using).

The distinction between polytheism and monotheism is therefore not just a matter of number. It's not that polytheists happen to believe in many gods and monotheists believe in just one. What polytheists mean when they talk of 'gods' is not transcendent reality, the source of all being, but a number of divine or semi-divine entities that may or may not exist within the world. They may fight, argue, fling down curses, make things, even mate with human beings; they may be visible or invisible or be representations of earthly activities or emotions, such as war, love or desire. But they belong within the same ontological frame of reference as you or me, the tree outside my window or the wind that whistles around my house. They are not, and never could be, the reason why all those things exist in the first place.

So where have we got to? I've suggested that the universal experience of wonder – that confession of ignorance as to why something exists at all and how it can stop us in our tracks – leads us to ponder the radical contingency of the world. I have also tried to demonstrate that the universe does not explain itself. Something simply cannot emerge out of nothing. There is a vast ontological distance between something (however small, simple and insignificant) and nothing, so a purely physical, materialist explanation of the universe or our existence doesn't make sense. The ultimate source of our existence cannot lie in some event or even person that kicked it all off in the first place and then is no longer needed – some ancient ancestor perhaps – because that event or person would require some explanation. As G. K. Chesterton once said, the materialist view of the world imagines 'an ever-increasing flood of water pouring out of an empty jug'.[7]

Might it be, after all, that there is something, or Someone, on the other side of all that we see around us, beyond all the fragile, normal reality that we experience every day? Contingent things cannot be explained by other contingent things; they can only be explained by something entirely different – something *necessary*. Something that cannot not be. And that is what the major religions of the world call God.

You never find in the Bible an argument for the existence of God. It just assumes God is there and develops a picture of the world based on that assumption. That is what you might expect if God cannot be proved. You just have to work out whether the world makes more sense on the assumption that there is such a God, rather than the assumption that there isn't. The point of this chapter is to try to open our eyes to the possibility that there may well be something, or even Someone, on the other side of our everyday experience, who brings out the true meaning and flavour of it, who makes sense of everything else and therefore tells us something about our place in it.

A final observation before the end of this chapter. One of the reasons why people sometimes don't believe in God is that they fear he will close down their options, as if they have to choose between God and anything else they enjoy, anything that might become a rival to him. In the film *The Lady in the Van*, the playwright Alan Bennett agrees to let an eccentric old lady called Mary Shepherd park her van in his drive for a few days. She stays for fifteen years. She also turns out to be a very gifted musician, daughter of a famous cellist, who had once wanted to join a convent. The problem was that, in the convent, music was strictly forbidden, as it was seen as a distraction from God. It was either God or music – you couldn't have both.

Many people suspect that God, if he exists at all, is out to stop any fun and we have to choose between him and things we enjoy in case it becomes a threat to him. This assumption makes the same category mistake that lurks behind the arguments we have looked at in this chapter. If God is another object in the world, taking up the same space as other things, then we might think, as Mary Shepherd did, that he competes for space with them, as it were. Yet, if God is not an object in the world, but is transcendent over it and immanent to it, then it is not a choice between God and good things. They are not in competition. God's presence brings out the goodness in all things – he is not a rival to them. That doesn't mean there aren't some choices to make, habits to avoid and priorities to fix, but it does help us to see how bringing God into a person's life might enhance the ordinary things of that life, bringing out its colour and flavour rather than crowding out all that is good and beautiful.

This might also begin to help us see how a belief in God might actually enhance our true selves rather than diminish them. Charles Taylor explains how our modern view of the world sees it as locked into an 'immanent frame'. It's like looking at a picture with a fixed, thick frame around it that tells you there is nothing outside the frame. With a materialist view of the world, everything worth looking at is within the frame, there is nothing beyond it.

But what if our experiences of wonder are cracks in that frame? What if they are signs that, after all, there is something outside the frame that breaks in from time to time and beckons us to explore it? If there is nothing beyond what we can see, if the world is enclosed by just the well-tried possibilities that the last chapter laid out – the consumerist individualism, whether of left or right, leading us to both personal and environmental crisis – then the future is bleak.

But if the awe that we experience at the staggering beauty of the natural world, strange coincidences that seem more than an accident or the delight at simple human kindness are cracks in the frame, letting light in from another realm, then maybe that opens up not just the possibility that this world is much bigger than we ever thought but also a whole different way of looking at life.

3
Why love is and isn't all you need

While growing up, Stuart Howarth was abused by his stepfather. Later in life, he tried to find reconciliation, yet when he tracked his stepfather down, encountering the same evil, abusive man, the meeting ended in a fight in which Stuart killed his tormentor. The inevitable prison sentence led to more violence and humiliation and, on release back into a society that offered no support, a cocktail of drugs and alcohol triggered suicide attempts before he began to recover with the aid of medical support and a loving partner, Tracy. When he wrote the story of his life, a powerful account of survival and resilience, Stuart described a young boy, eager to please, needing what every child needs, yet meeting with rejection and horrific abuse instead. The title he gave to his story says it all: *I Just Wanted to Be Loved.*[1]

This longing to be loved lies deep inside each of us, and it may just provide the clue to how to begin to answer many of the questions that we have been exploring so far. The last chapter opened up the possibility, maybe even the probability, of there being a transcendent source of everything that exists – a mind and a heart brooding on the other side of what we can see, invisible to our normal senses, but no less real. It also left us with another question: if there is such a Being, what might it be like? Are there any clues that might help us understand what or who it is? And might this longing for love lie at the heart of it?

Of course, I'm writing as a Christian, but it's a long way from believing that there is a God of some kind to identifying him, her or it as the Christian God. It was once said that '"God" is not a name, it is a job description.' The first step on the journey might be to recognize that there is a mystery beyond what our senses can immediately perceive – something we might call 'God'. The next step is to discover what or who that God is. If it doesn't sound too frivolous, it means working out who does the job of being God?

That might seem a fairly academic question, yet it matters a great deal. If this world is dependent on and emerges from something other than itself – if we ultimately come into being through this mysterious force we describe with the word 'God' – then surely it is of real interest to us to know what this force might be. It's a bit like someone abandoned as a child wanting to know what their parents were like, as it gives them some kind of clue to their own identity.

Or what about the experiences that give us goosebumps, the shudder in the night, the moments where your heart wants to burst with joy or freeze with fear, the occasions when you're aware that you're in the presence of something much bigger than you? Who, or what, is behind those moments? Might it just be that in those extreme emotions, someone is trying to get through to you? If they are, who is that 'someone'?

This is not just a modern question. Ancient myths, around at the time when the earliest books of the Bible were being written, had their own theories of how the world came into being. For example, the *Enuma Elish*, an ancient Babylonian text from the seventh century BC, gives a lurid account of how the world came into being. One God, Marduk, kills another called Tiamat and forms the heavens and the earth from the two halves of her corpse. Marduk then also murders Tiamat's husband, Kingu, using his blood to create humans so that they can perform menial tasks delegated to them by the gods. In other words, this world emerged out of primeval violence, and humans are slaves, bound to a miserable existence, subject to divine figures who have no real interest in them. If you believe that, then violence is inherent to the natural state of things. It's just normal. Moreover, there's no real reason not to treat other people as if they too are slaves, bound to be miserable, taking as little interest in them as the gods do.

Not many people believe that nowadays. We tend to believe that the origins of the universe lie in a huge, cosmic upheaval – the Big Bang. This idea emerged from the simple observation that other galaxies are spinning away from our own at enormous speed in all kinds of directions, exactly as if they had been propelled by some original explosive force. If that is true, then surely it matters to us to know what that force is.

Some scientists, straying into the territory of philosophy and theology, suggest that there is no particular purpose behind this event – it arises not from any prior consciousness or mind, but from the interaction of electromagnetic fields, virtual particles and the like, governed not by some divine intelligence, but by chance, even if the process of natural selection from that point onwards adds an element of purpose – the purpose of survival. Some accounts of the origins of the universe tell us that we emerged by random chance and we have survived so far because of an impersonal process of natural selection, which has meant that less well-adapted forms of life die out, and stronger ones, like us, survive.

But the question doesn't go away. Did this world arise out of violence, from mere chance or something else? As Macbeth laments his wife's death at the end of Shakespeare's play, he utters one of the most famous soliloquies in English literature:

> Life's but a walking shadow, a poor player
> That struts and frets his hour upon the stage
> And then is heard no more. It is a tale
> Told by an idiot, full of sound and fury
> Signifying nothing.

Is that it? Are we random flickers of life that appear for a short while and disappear almost as quickly?

When we get behind everything that we can see, or beyond the far edges of time itself, what do we find? If all that we see around us is contingent on something else – something necessary – what is that necessary thing like? The answer to that question surely matters, as it determines the way in which this world operates and how we understand ourselves within it. It also determines how we treat each other – are my neighbours, my friends or even my children the products of violence or random chance? Do they signify nothing? Are all forms of life ultimately in a competitive race for survival? If so, how will I treat them when the chips are down and my own well-being is threatened?

(Almost) all you need is love

I want to try to answer these questions by starting not with science, philosophy or even religion, but with another very common experience of life. The last chapter spoke about the idea of contingency. The basic idea was that everything we see around us is contingent, in that it might not have existed, and it is remarkable it is here at all. There is something else to be said about contingency, however. Contingent beings are not static. They are always growing or declining or developing in some way or another.

The theory of evolution by natural selection points us in this direction – that this world is in a constant state of flux and the whole natural world is a slowly evolving arena of life, developing from more simple to more complex forms. Trees, bushes and plants grow, flower and die. Animals are born, mature, age and also die, returning to the dust from which they came. Of course, the same is true of us human beings, but not only in a biological sense. True, we too are born and grow through childhood and adolescence into adulthood. We eventually grow older, our bodies decay and they die, just like plants and animals. Yet something goes on inside us as well, in a way that is more developed than in most other animal life. We learn, grow and mature not just physically but morally and intellectually as well. We develop particular characteristics, habits and instincts. The big question is what shape that maturity takes. Some people, over time, seem to grow, on the whole, wiser and better. Others, for whatever reason, grow into misshapen human beings, driven by jealousy, frustration or greed. What determines whether, on the inside, you grow healthy and wise or angry and mean?

'What determines whether, on the inside, you grow healthy and wise or angry and mean?'

When a child is born into the world, the very first thing that happens to him or her is that the baby's mother, father or whoever else happens to be present, smiles and looks on this new life with joy. Even the most unwanted babies, those who will only add to the complication of their parents' lives, still probably have this brief moment of being gazed at with love and delight. What happens from then on is anyone's guess. The child may continue to grow surrounded by the adoring love of her parents, wider family and community. Sadly, that doesn't always happen and the initial delight and surprise may give way to neglect or even abuse. What is certain is that whether a child knows love or its absence has a huge effect on the way he or she grows into adulthood.

'whether a child knows love or its absence has a huge effect on the way he or she grows into adulthood'

There may not be many things that we all agree on, but one of them is that we all need to be loved. In my job, I get to see many people at different stages of life, often at significant moments of birth, marriage, crisis or death. Most of these people have their scars, the harm that life has inflicted on them, some deeper than others. When

I come across people with nagging resentments or uncontrolled emotions, I can often guess what lies behind these symptoms. Some of them may have had life-changing injuries or suffered from economic depressions, job losses and so on, but such events don't seem to be the things that have the deepest effect on people. Most of the more complex or difficult people I've ever met are so because of one simple cause: a lack of love.

'Most of the more complex or difficult people I've ever met are so because of one simple cause: a lack of love.'

It may be that we never felt loved by our parents, so grew up never quite sure whether we had any value or were worth loving. It might have been difficult experiences at school, where the feeling that we were too fat, too ugly or too thick meant that we were never accepted and always felt left out of whatever was going on. It may be that we were rejected at a crucial point of life when we felt very vulnerable, whether by a marriage partner or a close friend. It could be a mix of all of these, but the bottom line is that most of our insecurities trace back to a sense that we have not felt loved. The more a person feels loved and lovable, the more he or she is likely to be a secure, stable and integrated person.

'The more a person feels loved and lovable, the more he or she is likely to be a secure, stable and integrated person.'

A recent study of people in the UK found that 1 in 10 did not consider themselves to have a close friend, and 1 in 5 said that they never or rarely felt truly loved. Of course, this isn't always related to reality. Psychologists tell us that our self-image is determined not by what we are, nor by what we think we are, nor even by what others think we are, but by what we think others think we are (I know that's complicated, but just think about it for a moment). In other words, however much we may be loved by others, if we don't think that we are, that is what counts. Many of us have a crippling inner voice that keeps telling us that no one could possibly love us because we are too much of a loser, too stupid, too worthless to love. That inner voice often goes back to negative experiences from childhood, especially the words and actions of those we depended on. If a parent looked on us as incompetent, lazy or worthless, we tended to believe them, just as we believed everything else they told us. We then internalized that voice, which became like one of those repeating recordings on a loop, triggered by anything negative happening to us or any criticism that came our way. Certainly, it is possible to overcome a lack of love in childhood, particularly by finding it later in life, yet it's hard to undo the damage. It's difficult to erase that soundtrack repeating in a person's memory, especially once it has gone deep into the psyche.

Now, the point of all this is not to offer any particular answers at this stage, but simply to point out the centrality of love to our human experience. If we know that we are loved, we can somehow cope with almost anything. If we feel ourselves to be unloved or unlovable, even the greatest riches, successes or triumphs can seem hollow. This isn't a particularly religious observation, but is something that we all sense to be true. It's not

> **'If we know that we are loved, we can somehow cope with almost anything. If we feel ourselves to be unloved or unlovable, even the greatest riches, successes or triumphs can seem hollow.'**

even particularly controversial. It just rings true to our experience. We spend our lives striving for success, for money, to look good, to get the perfect body, to become famous, yet, underneath, at the root of so many of those things is a desire to be loved or to make ourselves lovable. In fact, so often, the reason people want to become rich, successful or famous is because of a deficit of

'In fact, so often, the reason people want to become rich, successful or famous is because of a deficit of love.'

love. Somehow we convince ourselves that if we were rich and successful or famous, the people who matter to us would surely love us.

Learning to love

However, this is only half of it. We instinctively know how important it is to be loved, but we also know how important it is to be able to love other people in return. To be incapable of loving someone else is to miss out on some of the most satisfying parts of life. It is to fall short of being fully alive.

'To be incapable of loving someone else is to fall short of being fully alive'

I remember once getting to know a man who had been a homeless and rootless traveller for many years. He had been beaten up many times and had learnt to survive by using his wits and trusting nobody. I got to know him because one of my flatmates brought him home one day after finding him lying in a gutter, drunk and stoned at the same time. Many homeless people show great signs of compassion and groups of drifters can, at times, have a deeper sense of community than people in more respectable circles. However, in this case, trying to help was a nightmare. Any offer of help was seen as a threat, an attempt to cheat him out of something. He could never quite trust that anyone else might actually want to help him. He was perhaps the only person I've ever met who seemed incapable of loving anyone else. Thankfully, over time, he gradually changed, but at least he taught me one negative lesson: to be unable to love someone else diminishes our humanity.

The tests of love

We use the word 'love' a lot, yet before we go much further, it is worth trying to define what we mean by it. 'Love' is one of the most overused words in the world, and words that are worn out through overuse end up meaning very little.

C. S. Lewis, author of the Narnia Chronicles, once wrote a book called *The Four Loves*, where he contrasted four different meanings of the word – what he called Affection, Friendship, Eros and Charity.[2] These four overlap with one another, each can grow into the others, yet the greatest of them all, the one that underlies the others in all their best moments, is the last. It is what Lewis, after old translations of the Greek word *agape*, called Charity. This is simply the kind of love that seeks the welfare of someone else other than yourself – especially someone different from yourself. As Lewis put it, it is the love that, unlike the others, has 'no hunger that needs to be filled, only plenteousness that desires to give . . . it is wholly disinterested and desires simply what is best for the beloved . . . it enables (a person) to love what is not naturally lovable; lepers, criminals, enemies, the sulky, the superior and the sneering'.[3] And, more than that, what distinguishes this Judaeo-Christian idea of love from the romantic, erotic, touchy-feely sense it has acquired in more recent times is that it has very little to do with feelings. This kind of love is a series of actions and behaviours. How you feel about your neighbour or the person you are called to love has nothing to do with it – you might even dislike him or her intensely, but that doesn't mean you aren't still called to love that person.

This kind of love is easy to describe yet difficult to find. Hardly anyone admits to being selfish, opinionated or self-seeking. Love is not self-authenticating. Just because someone tells us that they love us, it doesn't actually mean they do – we have an instinct to ask how deep that love goes and how real it is. We want to test it. And that test

'Just because someone tells us that they love us, it doesn't actually mean they do'

is sacrifice. It's fairly easy to seek someone else's welfare as long as it doesn't damage your own. A wealthy person who earns five million pounds a year can appear generous by giving a £50 note to a homeless person once in while, but it involves no great sacrifice, because there will be more than enough money left to live on the rest of the time. The person who volunteers at a homeless centre once in a blue moon does something of value, but if it's on an evening when she wouldn't be doing much else, the gesture means comparatively little. If, however, someone regularly volunteers at the homeless centre, which means missing out on sharing a meal with friends or a ticket to a fantastic concert, that means a great deal more. If that same person volunteers at the centre when there is a real risk of violence or personal harm, yet does it anyway, that is getting closer to a true act of love. The real test of love is whether you continue to seek the welfare of someone else even when it costs you something, limits your own possibilities or possibly endangers your own life. During the coronavirus crisis that hit the world in 2020, the real heroes of the story were the nurses, doctors and volunteers who risked and sometimes gave their lives, making the ultimate sacrifice because of their willingness to care for those suffering from the disease. The test of real love is sacrifice.

'The test of real love is sacrifice.'

That doesn't mean love is a one-way street. Love does not demand the kind of endless self-giving that ends up with burnout, exhaustion or even abuse. Love is not entirely disinterested, in that the only person who benefits is the one who receives love. Although there is a definite element of sacrifice in love, learning to love is also good for you. Becoming the kind of person who is capable of creating relationships that are not just about you – where you make space for others to be, to breathe, to become the people they were made to be – has its own rewards. It brings a sense of community and belonging that self-centred egotism can never do. Even the ultimate self-sacrifice – giving up your life for a friend – might be preferable to survival with the lifelong guilt of having chickened out when presented with the supreme challenge of your life.

You've probably heard the command in the Bible, to 'love your neighbour as *yourself*'. In other words, loving others assumes a basic kind of self-love. Most of us take care of ourselves, ensuring that we have enough to eat and somewhere to sleep, looking after our health, making sure we have a few friends to spend time with and so on. We each have to assume responsibility for ourselves. We can't leave that to others by neglecting our own health, welfare or prospects. If we do, we are of little use to our neighbour who needs our care and attention. Loving my neighbour as myself requires that I look after myself, but also, crucially, that I do for the other person what I would do for myself. So if I take care of my own basic needs by ensuring that I have enough to eat, safe shelter and somewhere to sleep, access to healthcare, leisure time to enjoy and contact with good friends, then loving my neighbour (or my enemy) demands I make sure they have those things as well, as far as I am able and even if it involves some sacrifice on my part.

When we think of love, we often think that the highest form of love is romantic or erotic love: love for that one special individual whom we search for and, hopefully, find. Love means passion, heights of emotion or romantic feeling. Yet we don't often realize how cultural and time-bound such a view of love is. German sociologist Niklas Luhmann showed how love, understood as passionate attachment to one particular person and the almost sacred experience of 'being in love', was really only invented at the end of the Middle Ages. Before that, passionate love was seen as socially useless or even dangerous and, therefore, carefully regulated. He argued that the institutionalization of romantic love as a foundation for marriage is, in fact, a modern development. Before then, social relationships were determined by a person's station in life and a sense of duty. In the eighteenth century, however, such relationships were sentimentalized, or assessed in terms of personal emotions, so that 'being in love' began to trump all other considerations, such as loyalty to family, the duty owed to society and so on.[4] Since then, it has been woven into our expectation of life, the subject of countless romantic novels and Hollywood films.

Søren Kierkegaard, the Danish philosopher, loved to defy convention and wrote one of the most perceptive books on love ever published.[5] He suggested that the highest, best and purest form of love is not romantic love or even friendship, because they are based on accident or preference. If you are lucky enough to find someone you love and who loves you, that's great for you, but it doesn't always happen, and there are many people who never manage to find that person. Even more, this kind of love is determined by its object. We love someone who seems attractive or desirable to us, either as a lover or as a friend, but what about those who are not attractive or desirable to anyone? Are they ever loved? What happens when the person we have fallen in love with turns out not to be so attractive or desirable as we originally thought? What happens when a person gets flabby, becomes irritable in middle age, loses mental capacities or does something that we find objectionable or repulsive? Kierkegaard argues that what we usually call love is often nothing of the kind: 'one may make the mistake of calling love that which is really self-love: when one loudly protests that he cannot live without his beloved, but will hear nothing about love's task and demand.'[6] Love that is based on whim or a feeling of attraction is essentially unstable and fragile. Only love that is somehow independent of the object of love can be classed as the highest form of love. As Shakespeare put it:

Love is not love
Which alters when it alteration finds,
Or bends with the remover to remove.
O no! it is an ever-fixed mark
That looks on tempests and is never shaken.

Kierkegaard argues, therefore, that the highest and best form of love is not love for the person you are romantically attracted to, but love for your neighbour. In other words, it is love for the person who happens to live, work or play next to you, regardless of whether that person is attractive, lovable or desirable. True love is not about finding 'the one', the person who you find lovable, but about being able to love whoever has been put in your path each day. In Kierkegaard's words: 'the task is not to find the loveable object but to find the object already given or chosen loveable, and to be able to continue finding him loveable, no matter how they change'.[7]

We all understand the idea behind romantic love and friendship and, if we are lucky enough to have found someone to love in this way, whether as a lover or friend, it's easy to understand the attraction. Loving our neighbour, however, is much more difficult, largely because neighbours often are difficult. We don't choose our neighbours. They may be kind, thoughtful and pleasant. They may be angry, selfish and rude. Becoming the kind of person who is capable of loving our neighbours whatever they are like is a step and a stage beyond loving those we like or who like us.

Romantic love – the kind that C. S. Lewis called 'Eros' – is, on the one hand, absorbed with the beloved yet, on the other, wrapped up in the experience of being in love. The great Christian theologian St Augustine knew about this and wrote about it with as much self-perception as anyone. As he once put it, describing his experiences as an adolescent: 'I had never been in love and I longed to love. I sought an object for my love. I was in love with love.'[8] It's why so many songs or poems over the years are not so much about the beloved, but about the intoxicating experience of 'being in love' itself.

It's not that romantic love or friendship are of no value. They are precious – in fact, some of the best things that we experience. However, they are a kind of immature love. The emotions of romantic love may be the initial stirring that draws two people together, but it doesn't usually keep them together. Sometimes that intense feeling fades and nothing replaces it, which is when the relationship runs into trouble. In a healthy relationship, it matures into something more solid and reliable, less dependent on the attractiveness of the beloved. Most of us get saggy, wrinkled and set in our ways as we get older, so love needs to depend less on the feeling of attraction than on something that can grow within us: a capacity to love, to put someone else's needs above our own, regardless of who they are or what they look like.

Maturity as a human being means becoming this kind of person. Even if it doesn't sound the most attractive path of life for you, think about the sort of person you'd like to share a flat with or be married to. Someone who always put their own needs before yours would be hard to live with. Someone capable of always putting your needs before theirs, able to keep giving and wanting what is best for you – that, surely, would be the ideal partner.

'Someone capable of always putting your needs before theirs, able to keep giving and wanting what is best for you – that, surely, would be the ideal partner.'

Just in case anyone misunderstands this, it's not about being a doormat that other people simply walk over the whole time or someone who just vanishes into the background, taken advantage of by more assertive types. Love demands wisdom. Parents who give their kids chocolate, crisps and sugary drinks every time one of them demands some will end up with self-centred, undisciplined (and rather large) children. Doing what your neighbour, partner or children want you to do all the time is not necessarily loving, if what they want you to do is what would harm them. It takes quite a bit of experience of life, knowledge of people and how they work, as well as a lack of ego and the strength to say no sometimes, to judge what people really need to help them flourish.

Love is somehow central to our experience of being human. There are other experiences common to human life, such as pain, anxiety or hunger, but those are deficits – we know that they do not make us thrive, but instead diminish us. It is love that is essential to our flourishing. If we

'Love is somehow central to our experience of being human.'

do not think that we are loved, we cannot grow into healthy, happy people. If we do not learn to love, we also cannot grow into happy, healthy people. The first is key to the second. Those who know that they are loved are the best at knowing how to love others – they have the security to do it and also know a bit about what it looks like. If all this is true, it

'If we do not learn to love, we also cannot grow into happy, healthy people'

raises a real question mark about what we have always been told – that the secret of life is to ignore what everyone else tells you and be yourself. Maybe, instead, the secret of life is to love your neighbour? To do that means making a radical change to the way you view yourself.

In Chapter 1, we looked at what we tell ourselves these days – that we are autonomous individuals, each of us on a journey to discover our true selves by looking within to find out who we really are. A competitive consumerist individualism that enables us to acquire the means to achieve our self-chosen dream is the only option in town, even if it leads to increasing levels of anxiety, loneliness and environmental destruction.

Yet might this all be a big mistake? If our need to love and to be loved lies at the heart of our humanity, then maybe it is the ability to turn outwards towards the person who happens to be next to you right now, rather than inwards towards your own desires, that is the secret of true life and happiness? The capacity to ignore the nagging voice inside, the whining self that always wants its ego stroked, its needs instantly satisfied and, instead, to think yourself into what your neighbour needs, may turn out to be the secret of contentment after all. Maybe the route to true flourishing lies on the paradoxical path of self-denial, not self-discovery?

So far we have looked at our common experiences of wonder and love. There is a connection between them. When you know yourself to be loved, it is one of the most wonderful experiences possible. It is overwhelming. So, to return to the question at the end of the last chapter, as to what lies behind all the contingent things that surround us every day, does this experience of love give us a clue to what that is? If love is central to our experience of being human, then what might that tell us about the God who could be hidden, waiting for us behind what we see around us? And how would we ever find out what he is like?

4
Why the Big Bang has a face

Many religions and philosophies speak of love. Most of them have some version of the Golden Rule: do to others as you wish them to do to you. There are many definitions and descriptions of God. Yet at the heart of Christianity there is one definition that is simple yet utterly distinctive in its clarity: 'God is love'.[1]

I'm a Christian, born in a 'Christian' country (although that description may be past its sell-by date). If I had been born in a Muslim country, I might be writing a book about Islam, so why should we take these arguments seriously? Isn't the fact of religious pluralism an argument for relativizing the whole lot? The trouble is that this can't get us out of the search for the truth. Just because someone may adopt the beliefs of their society or upbringing has no bearing on whether they are true or not. A person living in 1930s Germany might well have believed the Nazi ideology – that does not make it true or excuse them from the responsibility of examining the truth or validity of what they were brought up to believe. Truth is not a function of geography. We have to do the work to examine the truth of any set of beliefs, whether religious or otherwise. And the best way to do that is not to examine some inner logical coherence of the system, but to ask whether it makes sense of things. Does it make sense of our experience of life? In this chapter I want to argue that Christianity does make sense of our experiences of wonder and love in a way that is deeply satisfying and enables us to live a good and well-spent life.

In the Qur'an, for example, Allah is described as many things: the Merciful, the Compassionate, the Just, the Bountiful, the Wise and so on, but in the traditional list of ninety-nine names for God, one thing is absent: the name of God as Love.[2] It is true that one of those names is Al-Wadoud – 'The All-Loving'. But this is to say that God loves, which is subtly but importantly different from saying that God IS love. It is one thing to say that God loves, as a kind of secondary activity, in the same way that he creates or smites or judges. It is another thing altogether to say that God *is* love in his very being.

Why, then, is love such a big deal in Christianity?

The maker in history

The Israeli–Palestinian conflict is one of the most complex political issues in the world today. It wasn't much different in the first century. That short strip of land at the eastern edge of the Mediterranean had been a major thoroughfare for wandering traders, armies and warlords for centuries, as it was the main land route between northern Africa to the south and Asia and Europe to the north and west. Whoever occupied this land could control trade routes and thus levy taxes on anyone travelling between these major landmasses. Over the years it had been occupied by Canaanites, Babylonians, Assyrians, Persians and Greeks. However, a small group of settlers, tracing their roots back to the mists of prehistory, the *'Apiru*, or Hebrews as they came to be known, had also laid claim to this small space of fertile coastal plains and desert hills, believing that God had promised it to them.

In the first century AD, the Jews had recently experienced a brief period of control in what they always considered their land, having got rid of the Seleucids, a Greek regime that ruled the country at the tail-end of Alexander the Great's empire. It wasn't long, however, before they lost out yet again to the next major world empire that came along – the Romans. The Jews deeply resented the Romans as mere occupiers of a land they believed God had given them, and thought of these invaders as an enemy who would surely soon be expelled. As always when land and control is disputed, there were factions, tension, rebellion, riots, unrest – the symptoms of an uneasy nation.

There were the Sadducees, religious aristocrats in a society that took religion very seriously, a priestly caste in cahoots with sophisticated Greek culture, yet also following the old traditions of Israel and who looked down on other groups who didn't share their exalted status. The Pharisees were religious puritans, distrusting King Herod and his new Temple, seeking to avoid contamination with a pagan Gentile world. There were the Essenes, a separatist group, a bit like the Amish, who had left the corruption and compromise of Jerusalem and set up camp in the desert waiting for the Messiah to come to rescue them. Then there were the Zealots, who thought the only answer to Roman occupation was armed resistance.

At the heart of the tussles for control of *Palestina*, as the Romans called this region, was the city of Jerusalem, the capital, the place where the Jews believed that God dwelt in the great Jewish Temple, a massive building that dominated the city and that had recently and controversially been rebuilt by the mixed-race (half-Jewish, half-Idumean) Herod the Great.

One fateful Passover day, into this political turmoil came a rough peasant rabbi, riding into Jerusalem after a long walk down from his base near the Lake of Galilee to the north, with a small retinue of followers not far behind. For a few years he had been causing a stir with reports of miracles, controversial ideas and even rumours that he had brought people back from the dead. His announcement that a new era called the 'kingdom of God' was coming was greeted with great excitement, especially by the poorer end of the spectrum of Jewish society, and by some of the more radical groups around. Yet it also seemed a direct challenge to the kingdom of Caesar, the kingdom of Herod or the religious establishment, busy trying to appease the Roman authorities in case they closed down Jewish worship altogether.

Jesus, or Yeshua, to give him his Jewish name, was very different from any other religious figure you may have heard of. Out of all the great religious leaders of the world, Jesus seems to have been the only one whose main activity during his public life was healing the sick. If the Gospels are anything to go by, he spent a lot of his time straightening bent limbs, making blind people see again, curing deafness and bringing peace of mind to those troubled by mental or spiritual illness.[3] While there are miracle stories associated with Muhammad, such as his night journey from Mecca to Jerusalem and then to heaven and back, they are very limited and don't include healing miracles, perhaps out of a desire not to overshadow the primary 'miracle' in Islam, which is of course the giving of the Qur'an itself. Gautama the Buddha is said to have possessed various superhuman powers and abilities, notably various kinds of telepathy, divine vision and so on, but he refused to perform miracles, including miracles of healing, saying instead, 'I dislike, reject and despise them.'[4]

Reading the Gospels, however, it is remarkable how much of them is taken up with an account of Jesus' mysterious supernatural activity, doing things no ordinary human could do. The writers depict him walking across the surface of a lake, feeding several thousand people with just a few bread rolls and some sardines and even resuscitating corpses on occasion. If there were just a few of these stories, we might just dismiss them as a bit of naïve pre-modern exaggeration, but they are so much a central part of the story, woven through it at every point, we have to take them seriously.

People often think of Jesus as a great teacher, whose ideas are the most important thing and the miracle stories are just a bit of ancient myth, which you can take or leave. Yet the way his story is told in the Gospels doesn't work like that. He was a teacher of wisdom to his closest followers and to the crowds but, rather than the miracles being adverts to draw a crowd or even illustrations of his teaching, it actually seems to be the other way around. It seems that his whole life was not a set of philosophical musings, but a constant battle with all that diminishes and destroys human life – sickness, injustice and death.

Those early skirmishes came to a head when he finally arrived in Jerusalem, the religious capital of the nation and the seat of Roman power in Palestine. Within a few days of his arrival, Jesus of Nazareth was dead. Arrested, tried and convicted of sedition, he was treated to the most cruel of all deaths devised by a particularly cruel regime – crucifixion, which involved a slow suffocation as the victim, nailed to a cross, gradually became unable to lift his pain-wracked body to take in another breath.

Yet, within a week of his death, the rumour had begun to spread that he had been seen alive, and the body that had been flayed by Roman whips and hung lifeless on a wooden plank kept appearing to some of his followers, not in some kind of hallucinatory dream, but real. There was no chance that he had somehow survived the ordeal – the Romans were very good at execution and didn't make mistakes with this sort of thing. Before long, something quite unimaginable started to happen – people began worshipping a crucified man.

You might think that the worship of Jesus as God's Son was something that only developed many centuries later, in a kind of religious version of Chinese whispers, where an ordinary teacher gets transformed into a god after many generations of increasingly exaggerated claims. In this case, that theory just doesn't work. Even at the earliest stages of the telling of the Jesus story, there is evidence that his followers believed, and he himself thought, that he was not just an ordinary rabbi, but was somehow in a unique relationship with God. There is his strange way of speaking about having 'come into the world', implying that he was conscious of having come from somewhere other than the earth – an odd way for an ordinary human being to refer to his origins. Then there is his habit of claiming to forgive other people's sins. If you tell a lie about me, I could forgive you. What I can't do is forgive someone else if they tell a lie about you – that's between you and them, nothing to do with me. The only person who might be qualified to forgive that person (besides you, of course) is God, the one who upholds the moral structure of the cosmos, whose job it is, supposedly, to forgive sins. It's no surprise when those who heard this claim objected, 'Why does this fellow speak in this way? It is blasphemy! Who can forgive sins but God alone?'[5]

He thinks that the angels belong to him,[6] he accepts the worship of his followers, whereas a true rabbi would, of course, deflect all worship on to God alone.[7] His chosen way to enter Jerusalem, riding on the back of a donkey, was no act of deferential humility, because it's exactly what the Old Testament prophets said God's chief representative, his chosen king, would do when he came to rescue Jerusalem.[8] I could go on, but there's too much here, too many strange things said and done by Jesus to let him pass as just a normal rabbi or prophet, pointing the way to God.

It only took a few short years for his followers, even those who had known him personally, to call him things like 'the image of the invisible God, the firstborn of all creation',[9] 'the exact imprint of God's very being',[10] or 'God the only Son, who is close to the Father's heart'.[11] You could understand that kind of exaggeration a few centuries later, but not when the memory of the flesh-and-blood human being who ate fish with them, grew a beard and had to pee like everyone else was still fresh in the mind.

Unlike Muhammad, who Muslims always considered a prophet (and still do), teaching the way of God, delivering the word of God in the Qur'an, Christians quickly began to think of Jesus not as a messenger of the word of God, but as the Word of God itself in human flesh. He was not just a teacher of the truth; he was the Truth. He did not just show the way, he was the Way. Most prophets, whether in the Old Testament or in other religions altogether, are at pains to draw attention away from themselves towards their message. With Jesus it is different. When John, one of Jesus' closest disciples, came to sum up the significance of his appearance among them, he used amazingly bold language: 'the Word became flesh and lived among us'.[12] In other words, Jesus does not just point away from himself to the God who stands behind everything that exists. Because of the impact he had on them, the early Christians came to believe that he is the complete expression of that God in human form. As G. K. Chesterton put it, in Christianity we find 'the loud assertion that the mysterious maker of the world has visited his world in person'.[13] This was the Creator of flesh appearing in flesh. The Maker in the dirt.

'This was the Creator of flesh appearing in flesh. The Maker in the dirt.'

Of course, many religious figures have dispensed wisdom, acted out of compassion, even performed the odd miracle. Yet there is one further and overriding reason why the early Christians started saying such astonishing things about Jesus – and that is that no other religious leader had been both executed and then had that verdict reversed by being raised from the dead.

We'll look at this claim a bit more in the next chapter, but it does help to explain why Christians believe that this crucified Jewish teacher and worker of miracles is the clue to the identity of whatever force it was that created the world. His character, actions and emotions are a window into the character, actions and emotions of God. When those earliest Christians went further to describe that character, they were driven back to this one word: Love.

Love in the dirt

When you get time – perhaps when you finish this chapter – just look up one of the four Gospels in the Bible and start to read.[14] They offer extraordinary pictures of someone who has the security and inner strength just to keep giving life and love to whoever crosses his path. It is exactly the kind of love that we saw C. S. Lewis describing in the last chapter, the kind that has 'no hunger that needs to be filled, only plenteousness that desires to give . . . [It] desires simply what is best for the beloved . . . it enables him to love what is not naturally lovable.'[15]

This was compassion with a difference. It not only expressed solidarity and sympathy, as most of us might do; it actually changed things. The power of love that flowed out of Jesus was so strong that it healed sick people, whether damaged in mind or body. In Jesus' day, one of the most common sights in the gutters by the roadside were the lepers, ostracized by everyone because it was believed they were both infectious and ritually unclean. But when Jesus touched them (horrors!), instead of Jesus catching leprosy as everyone expected, the reverse happened – lepers somehow became healed of their disease. Rather than bad infection passing from them to him, good infection flowed from him to them. This was true love – love in the gutter.

Then there was Zacchaeus – the filthy rich inland revenue official, despised by just about everyone as an agent of the occupying Roman power and as a cheat, as many of his fellow tax collectors were. The equivalent in our day would be the reviled loan shark, preying on the poor by charging extortionate interest. On visiting Zacchaeus's home town of Jericho – in contrast to everyone else, who refused to speak to him and treated him as a pariah – Jesus made a bee-line for this loathsome man out of the whole crowd gathered to see him and invited himself to his home, a place no one else would be seen dead in (I did say that this kind of love has little to do with feelings of attraction). The result was dramatic – Zacchaeus resolved to give away 50 per cent of his bank balance and promised repayment and more to anyone who he might have cheated or demanded extra cash from in the past.[16]

Then there was the woman caught having sex with someone else's husband and summoned by the religious police to face justice. Just as the (presumably male) crowd begin to pick up stones for the public execution that her crime was thought to deserve in that culture, they turn to Jesus for his expected confirmation of the sentence passed on her. Enigmatically, he bends down and starts scratching something in the dust with his finger while they wait for his verdict. 'OK,' he says, 'fair enough, let's stone her. Who is going to be first? I have an idea – why don't we find someone who has never had a lustful thought towards a woman like this and let them start . . .?' Silence. Slowly the stones drop to the ground and the crowd slips away, leaving just the woman and Jesus. 'I don't condemn you,' he says. 'Just go – make a new start, but mind you don't get into this mess again.'[17]

This power of love that flowed out of Jesus, even, on a couple of occasions, brought people back from the dead, such as the time Jesus and his friends bumped into a funeral procession. The young man who was being carried in the open coffin was the only son of a woman who had already lost her husband some time before. Jesus, it seems, was deeply grieved in his own spirit at the heart-rending sobbing of the mother, now left alone and defenceless in the world. He reaches out his hand and touches the bier, tells him to get up, upon which the boy suddenly sits up and begins to talk. Jesus helps him down, takes him to his mother and the joy that follows is left to our imagination.[18]

There are numerous stories like this throughout the Gospels. Jesus gives a name to this kind of thing. He calls it the 'kingdom of God' – the state where things happen the way God wants them to, the way they were always meant to be in the beginning before everything got twisted, when everything gets wrapped up in love. The point of the early Christians' belief that Jesus was God's Son, the 'reflection of God's glory and the exact imprint of God's very being',[19] is that these things that Jesus did reveal God to us. Forget the angry old man with the white beard shaking his fist and flinging curses on whoever irritates him – that is Thor or Zeus, not the God of the Christians. Forget the impassive despot dispensing good fortune and bad, depending on whatever mood he is in. When Jesus heals a leper, welcomes a pariah, forgives an adulterer, gives a grieving widow her son back from the dead, that is what God does. It's not that God doesn't get angry. He does. But he gets angry at everything that threatens to dismantle and destroy the good things he has made – and that includes the pride, envy and greed that diminishes us, breaks our friendships and destroys our (or better, his) planet.

'in the face of Jesus we see the Love that created the world'

Christians believe that it is in the face of Jesus that we see the Love that created the world perfectly expressed in human flesh and blood. It is the Big Bang with a face and a name. If you tried to put God, the Creator of the world, into an ordinary human life, this is what it would look like. It's what

'It is the Big Bang with a face and a name.'

it did look like. This was not one of the regular appearances of divine beings in mortal form, the staple of many Greek myths, but

the God behind the gods, the mysterious source of everything that exists, appearing before their very eyes, no longer invisible but the visible 'image of the invisible God'.[20] You couldn't tell immediately – there was no obvious halo behind his head or phosphorescent glow to his flesh (apart from one dramatic occasion when a small group of his closest friends suddenly saw a luminous, brilliant light shining out of him on the top of a mountain).[21] You could shake his hand as with any other human being, but if you had eyes to see it, when you did, you were shaking the hand of God.

Of course, it took the early Christians several centuries to work out the full implications of the mind-bending possibility that God had appeared on earth, like an author suddenly appearing in the middle of his own novel. But the basic outlines of the belief are there from very early days. Christians say that God is love not because they think it would be convenient if he was, and certainly not because the world is a nice place and the creation as we experience it points unambiguously to a good and kind God (see the next chapter for that one). They say it because they believe that God has revealed his hand or, more exactly, shown us his face – and it is the face of Jesus, the face of compassion turned towards a grieving widow, a despised tax official, a guilty woman – people just like you and me in our worst moments.

St Paul once visited Athens and noticed an altar with a dedicatory inscription. It simply said 'To an unknown god'. It gave him an idea for a speech in the famous Areopagus, the centre of government and debate in the city. His opening line was bold, to say the least: 'What therefore you worship as unknown, this I proclaim to you.'[22] This 'unknown god' – whatever it was that brought the universe into being – we now have a clue as to what it is like and who it is.

On 20 July 1969, two men landed on the moon and started to collect samples. Until then, throughout human history, people had looked up at the moon and wondered what it was made of. Even after the invention of the telescope, when it was possible to analyse it more closely, we were still guessing. It wasn't until someone actually stepped on the moon, bent down, put some moon rock and dirt into a container and brought it back home to earth that we could tell what the moon was really made of. We no longer had to guess – we had reliable information about the moon because we could touch it, analyse it, study it for ourselves. It's not a perfect analogy but it helps us understand what Christians mean when they call Jesus the 'Son of God'. One of the earliest Christian writers wrote: 'what we have seen with our eyes, what we have looked at and touched with our hands, concerning the word of life – this life was revealed, and we have seen it and testify to it'.[23] Just as scientists were able to see and handle 'real moon' in the rocks and dust they had in their hands, so in the actions and attitudes of Jesus we could see 'real God'.

'Just as scientists were able to see and handle 'real moon' in the rocks and dust they had in their hands, so in the actions and attitudes of Jesus we could see 'real God'.'

Yet there is a further reason why Christians place Love as central to the character of the God who made the world.

One and three

This belief about Jesus messed with the heads of good monotheistic Jews such as the earliest followers of Jesus. It led to the notoriously complicated (but wonderful – wait for it) idea of the Trinity. This was the result of a process of deep and intricate thinking by the earliest Christians – a process that took around four hundred years, trying to make sense of the difference it made to their view of God, if they believed that God had appeared in history in human form. If God was the Creator, sustaining the world from moment to moment, and yet was also right in front of them in the person of Jesus, and was also mysteriously experienced among them as they met together as a group after Jesus had died, risen again and ascended, how on earth could you make sense of all this and speak about one God any longer?

The answer is that they couldn't. They had to come up with something more complex, but ultimately more satisfying and true to what they had seen and heard. The result was the doctrine of the

Trinity – the idea that God is still one God, not three gods, but that oneness is made up of Father, Son and Holy Spirit, three distinct persons, yet sharing exactly the same essential nature.

Now this all may sound difficult to understand, yet stay with me, because it takes us deeper into the mystery of being and the centrality of love.

At the heart of this idea of the three persons in the oneness of God is the reality of Love. When Jesus spoke of his relationship with God, who he called his Father, the key note that he struck was that of a deep, abiding, powerful love: 'The Father loves the Son' is a repeated refrain.[24] And when he speaks to God, who he calls his Father, the conversations breathe an atmosphere of utter trust and intimacy, even when it seems that his Father is asking him to go through the most terrifying suffering. The Holy Spirit that Jesus promised to his followers is also described as the 'Spirit of Love'.[25]

In some philosophies and religions, such as Stoicism and Shintoism for example, the creation is part of God, an extension of his being. Any monotheistic creed, however, draws a strict distinction between God and his creation. For Christianity, Islam and Judaism (the main monotheistic religions), the creation is not divine, but it is something that God chose to bring into being, something different from himself. Moreover, God existed before the creation. In Islam, with its strict monotheism, before the world was created, there can only have been God on his own. Putting it simply and bluntly, within a simple monotheism, before the creation, God had nothing to love, because there was nothing other than God. Once the creation had come into being, then, of course, it could become the object of divine love, but then love is something that God does as a kind of secondary activity, rather than something that is at the core of his very being. That is why the Qur'an is logically quite correct not to add the name of 'Love' to the ninety-nine names of God.

Christianity, however, is monotheism of a different kind than the sort found in Islam or Judaism. Because of this belief that Jesus is God in human flesh, and their belief that they experienced the on-going spirit of Jesus when they met together, even after he had left them, Christians began to say they still believe in one God, but also that God is made up of three persons – Father, Son and Holy Spirit, who all share the same essential nature. But here I want to make one simple point. If God is, and always was, Father, Son and Holy Spirit, eternally bound together in relationships of love, then even before the creation, even before there was anything other than God, God *was* love, because Father, Son and Holy Spirit were 'in love' with one another long before the world came into being. Strict monotheism can say that God loves, as one of a range of activities or emotions that God may indulge in, but it cannot say that God *is* love.

In the same way, polytheism – the idea that there are numerous gods – cannot ultimately say that God is love either. If there are many gods, all with different characteristics and personalities, such as in Greek mythology or even in Hinduism, it becomes impossible to say anything definitive about God or even about ultimate reality, other than the rather dull observation that at the end of the day there is just difference. In Greek mythology, there may be a god of love (Eros or Aphrodite for example), but he or she might sit alongside a god of beauty or war or knowledge or drunkenness. The Greeks, likewise, could never have come up with a statement like 'God is Love'. The idea of the Trinity may be hard to get your head around, but para-doxically, it is only this kind of God that enables us to make such a remarkable and counter-intuitive statement.

Putting the pieces together

Our deep and fundamental need to be loved and to love is not just incidental, one of a number of basic longings, but is our primary need. Yes, we need food, shelter, education, clean water and all the other basic requirements for life, but if we have all those yet do not have love, then we end up phys-

'Our deep and fundamental need to be loved and to love is not just incidental but is our primary need.'

ically satisfied, yet emotionally and spiritually stunted. True, if we have love without all those other things, it's hard to survive, but if we are loved, then those who love us – whether parents, friends or strangers – will usually ensure that we have food, shelter and the rest. Love will provide for our physical needs, but our physical needs don't in themselves provide love.

Love is fundamental to our experience of life. And out of all the various religions and philosophies in the world, it is Christianity that speaks most centrally and powerfully of love. It has always seemed to me that there is something uncannily fitting about this. We each have a desperate need for love and long for it throughout our lives, and in Christianity we get this declaration, not just that we need love, but we were made for love, and that love is exactly what we find coming towards us from the other side of existence and visible in the face and hands of Jesus Christ.

But can't atheists also believe in love? After all, the same John Lennon who penned the great secular anthem 'Imagine' also wrote 'All you Need is Love'. Perhaps you can retain an ethic of love, particularly for the vulnerable and poor, alongside a humanist world view – having your sceptical cake and eating it? Yet it's far from clear that you can. The German philosopher Friedrich Nietzsche (1844–1900) was perhaps the critic of Christianity who understood it best. And he realized that this didn't work. Jettisoning the belief in a God revealed in a crucified man also meant jettisoning the belief that the weak and vulnerable were worthy of love and attention. He understood the nature of Christianity and its consequent command to care for the poor and the frail – and he hated it. He wrote of 'the seductive, intoxicating, anaesthetising and corrupting paradox of the "crucified God"',[26] despising it for its regard for the weak, its holding back of the strong, its ethic of self-denial rather than giving in to our deepest instincts: 'I regarded the inexorable progress of the morality of compassion, which afflicted even the philosophers with its illness, as the most sinister symptom of the sinister development of our European culture.'[27] He knew darn well that the virile, blood-soaked pagan Roman Empire, the culture that he admired so much more than the Jewish or the Christian faith that, much to his regret, supplanted it, had no such sentimental attachment to the weak.

If you believe the world emerged not out of love but chance, that the basic rule of survival is that those able to adapt and change always outlive those who cannot, this gives no particular reason to care for the weak and frail. Just asserting that human beings have value does not make it so, and certainly gives no grounds for arguing with a different mindset that also asserts some humans (of a particular skin colour, ethnicity or gender) are worth more than others. Of course, this isn't to say that atheists don't care for people – many are heroic in their compassion and love – yet it is to suggest that they are perhaps unwittingly drawing on the Christian roots of their culture rather than on something authentically drawn from secular or humanist assumptions. As many others have pointed out, if the Western mind feels an instinct of compassion for the poor and vulnerable that is because of the Christian revolution that took place over two thousand years ago – it is by no means obvious.[28]

To put it a little differently, we touched earlier on the Big Bang, the ancient cataclysm that gave birth to our universe, planets propelled into existence by some prehistoric explosive force, and wondered about what that force might have been. Christianity gives an answer to that question: if Jesus really is the vital clue to the character of the God who made the world, then the power that brought the universe into being, the driving energy of the universe that runs through the world like the words through a stick of rock, is none other than Love.

Once you understand that, the whole world looks different. The planet we live on is not an object, some inert lump of cosmic dust, but a gift given by a Lover, a garden for us to enjoy (which is the root meaning of the word 'Eden'). The earth beneath our feet, the roof over our heads, the air we breathe, lakes, flowers, rivers and mountains, are not random physical phenomena, but expressions of the love that propelled the universe into being. If the world was born out of love, it explains why we so badly need love and why we thrive in its presence and shrivel in its absence.

Now, let me say it again: no one can prove the existence of God and this isn't an argument that tries to do it by the back door. We are dealing in probabilities and likelihoods here and what makes most sense of our experience of life. Just as our experience of wonder points to some mysterious but very real source beyond all that we see, feel and touch, our experience and need for love points to the nature of that source to be just that: a love that speaks to us across eternity. The two pieces of the jigsaw puzzle fit exactly.

One day, Jesus was asked which is the greatest commandment. Perhaps today we would put that question differently: what is the purpose of human life? He did not say, 'be yourself' or 'believe in yourself'. He said: '"You shall love the LORD your God with all your heart, and with all your soul, and with all your mind, and with all your strength." The second is this, "You shall love your neighbour as yourself."'[29]

Just as in our day we have different varieties of competitive consumerist individualism, in Jesus' day the many religious groupings offered competing variations on the way to keep the nation safe and secure. Sadducees, Pharisees, Essenes, Zealots all had their way of dealing with outsiders – patronizing them, avoiding them, rejecting them or fighting them. Jesus alone took the radical, and so difficult and costly, step of suggesting people try to love them.

According to the Christian faith, that is what you are here for. Whether you become famous, earn lots of money, travel the world and collect amazing experiences is all secondary and relatively trivial against the real purpose of your life, which is to learn to live in tune with the power that gave birth to the world, to live with the grain of the universe, to become somebody capable of love. And again, to avoid misunderstanding, this is not primarily about feeling warm thoughts about others, but about the slow, steady, patient ability to surrender your own comfort and prosperity for the sake of someone else – not just your friends and family, but your neighbour and, even more, your enemies. It is to extend to your neighbour exactly the kind of care that you would give to yourself and to find in doing so that you thrive and flourish – finding yourself by losing yourself.

What Jesus offered people at the time, and still does today, is a different way of seeing life and living it. Instead of the wearying effort to find ourselves by looking inside at our ever-changing and unstable emotions or desires, it suggests we **'we will find ourselves in the** will find ourselves in the relation-**relationships we create a** ships we create – with the God **way of self-discovery not** who made us, with the people we **through being yourself, but** are close to, with those who come **through learning to love'** across our path each day and even, perhaps, those who don't like us. It offers a way of self-discovery not through being yourself, but through learning to love.

Yet this leaves an obvious question that might have occurred to you already. This world doesn't always look like the creation of a God of love. The existence of suffering and pain in the world is, for many people, a huge stumbling block to believing in God, or, at least, in a God who is supposed to be love. Sooner or later, we have to address the age-old problem of evil.

5
Why evil exists and why it can't be explained

On 14 June 2017, I awoke, as I normally do, around 6 a.m. As I stumbled towards the bathroom, I picked up my phone and noticed a direct message from a local radio station. It asked whether I had any comment to make about the fire. What fire? I thought, as I quickly looked at the BBC website to work out what they might be talking about. I discovered something we all now know: that a blaze had broken out in a tower block in west London and many casualties were feared. I quickly realized that Grenfell Tower stood in one of the parishes that I am responsible for as the local bishop.

I decided to get there as quickly as possible, not quite sure what I could do to help, but wanting at least to be present to support those who were in the thick of it. I spent much of that morning at the base of the Tower, listening to the harrowing stories of firefighters who were going in and out of a still-burning building that looked as if it could collapse at any minute, while they stepped over bodies, enduring unbearable heat. Over the subsequent weeks and months, I came to know several of the families who had escaped or had lost close relatives in the fire. I can still hear the devastated weeping of one family as they heard the news that their five-year-old boy had not made it out of the Tower.

It wasn't long before the cry for justice and for answers began to be heard. On one level, it could be put down to human error or negligence. Somehow, people had made decisions that rendered this tower block vulnerable to such a devastating fire and we needed a right and proper process to try to work out who was responsible and what should be done about it. On one occasion, during one of the many media interviews I gave at the time, I was asked whether this tragedy shook my faith in God and whether I could give any explanation as to why God could allow such things to happen. The assumption behind the question was that such events must question the idea that God, if he exists, could in any way be described as good, given that he either makes such things happen in his world or, at the very least, allows them to happen.

The problem of suffering is one of the most common reasons why people don't believe in God or perhaps give up on him. It's one that religious people often don't like to talk about, because it seems an insuperable problem that they wish would somehow go away. I have come to think, however, that alongside the experience of wonder and our need for love, our experience of suffering and trouble is another clue that helps us make sense of the world we are in. The

'our experience of suffering and trouble is another clue that helps us make sense of the world we are in'

answer I gave to the journalist during the interview was that, in a strange way, the tragedy made me trust in God even more than I did before. This chapter tries to explain why.

Now, I know that what I'm trying to do here can sound a bit sterile. The problem of evil is not just a philosophical problem. It is a deeply personal one. The agony of a parent who goes to the cot to find their child no longer breathing, a whole village wiped out by a tsunami, a long struggle with crippling depression, a viral pandemic that kills thousands of people across the planet: the amount of pain and suffering happening all over the world at any moment completely outstrips our capacity to imagine let alone comprehend it. Yet we have to try to think about it, because for Christians like me who believe in God or for anyone contemplating doing so, it is a problem to reconcile a good God with a broken world. If he made it, he's ultimately responsible for it. And at first glance he hasn't done a very good job.

Strangely enough, until comparatively recently, the existence of suffering was hardly ever really seen as a valid objection to the existence of God. You can read any book of Christian theology written before the seventeenth century and no one seriously raises it as a problem. What has changed? It's not that people in the past were a bit simple, whereas we are clever enough to recognize that there may be a logical problem in simultaneously believing in a good God who created the world *and* the existence of evil. It's more that our general approach to life has changed. With the Industrial Revolution, the rise of technology, the advance of medicine and so on, we now tend to think that if there is a problem, we can fix it. Suffering is a problem, so surely we should be able to sort it out or, if *we* can't, God should. We also tend to assume now that we have a right to 'life, liberty and the pursuit of happiness', as the American Declaration of Independence put it. Anything that threatens those rights, such as illness, poverty or mishap, is just wrong and someone – either God or the government – is to blame.

In earlier times of human history, however, suffering was simply accepted as part of the way things were. Some, of course, reflected on suffering and how to deal with it, such as the story of Job in the Bible, the story of a wealthy man who loses everything in a series of disasters, but even that book does not consider suffering a reason for atheism. It is essentially a long conversation between the unfortunate Job and his well-meaning friends about why such things happen and how to deal with them. It never occurs to them that the tragedies that happen to Job might mean God doesn't exist.

These days, however, it usually comes up sooner or later in any conversation about religion, especially if Christians start talking about a God of love, as I've been doing in the last chapter. Over the history of philosophy and religion, many different answers have been proposed to the question of why God allows bad things to happen in his world, but they can broadly be grouped into three basic approaches.

The price of freedom?

One set of answers revolves around the exercise of human free will. God has given us freedom, so the argument goes, because otherwise we would be robots, our choices would be meaningless and, therefore, we would lack any dignity or responsibility. God wants a world where his creation responds to him with love, which necessarily requires freedom – love that is forced on us is abuse, not love.

But this arrangement comes with the risk that this very freedom may be used to destroy rather than to create, to harm rather than help. Much of the suffering in the world can therefore be traced back to human choices, whether the petty wounds we inflict on each other through careless words, the injustices of economic systems that fail to provide food for the hungry or medicine for the sick, the racism that blights the lives of millions or the carelessness or neglect that leads to a fire that kills innocent people. It is logically impossible, even for an omnipotent God, to create a world of free creatures who never choose evil. However, God decided, so the argument goes, that it would be better to create the world with the possibility of evil than not create it at all.

This line of thinking explains a great deal of the suffering we experience. To be betrayed by someone you thought cared for you, to have a friend tell lies about you, to be insulted, shouted at, trolled on social media or just ignored and neglected is deeply painful. Many of the routine day-to-day struggles we have to deal with are down to other people's (and our own) greed, selfishness or jealousy. Famines are exacerbated, perhaps even caused, by our inability to share the resources of the world we live in. Diseases are spread by our reckless failure to ensure proper hygiene. And this is entirely because we live in a connected world.

In previous eras in the West, we were perhaps guilty of forgetting our integral relationship, not just with each other, not even just with God, but with the earth itself. As recent thinking on our relationship with the environment reminds us, we do not live in isolation from this planet – what we do affects the earth, and what happens to the earth affects us. Sunsets and mountain waterfalls can amaze us. Tsunamis and earthquakes can destroy us. At the same time, gardening and conservation can nurture the planet, carbon emissions and toxic waste can destroy it. Small acts of goodness can lead to remarkable creativity, yet equally small acts of anger, vanity or cruelty not only harm those they affect directly, but have the potential to damage the whole cosmic order. The balance of nature is such a delicate and finely tuned thing that careless human choices can have catastrophic effects. Overfishing of sardines or anchovies can remove key sections of the food chain in the oceans, leading to the elimination of species that depend on them for their own survival. Bottom trawling, which sweeps ocean floors with nets, can destroy the ecosystem that gradually builds up in such remote places, leading to the disturbance of the delicate web of life.

Human action, or inaction, lies at the heart of much of the hurt and damage we experience.

It is hard to blame God for evil that comes about as a result of human choices. The Grenfell Tower fire was the result of a cocktail of human error – building regulations ignored, safety disregarded, mistakes made in the immediate response. Human choice plays a large part, not just in major disasters like that one, but also in the regular day-to-day suffering that people everywhere have to endure.

But such an argument doesn't satisfy everyone. In 2015, Stephen Fry caused a social media sensation after an interview with the Irish broadcaster Gay Byrne. When asked what he would say to God if he met him after death, he replied:

> I'll say: bone cancer in children, what's that about? . . . Yes, the world is very splendid, but it also has in it insects whose whole life-cycle is to burrow into the eyes of children and make them blind. They eat outwards from the eyes. Why did you do that? Why? Why did you do that to us? You could easily have made a creation where that didn't exist. It is simply not acceptable.

Ivan Karamazov, Fyodor Dostoyevsky's character from the novel *The Brothers Karamazov*, in a long monologue similarly rejects God because no amount of freedom or goodness or even beauty can make up for the amount of suffering and evil in the world. If the bargain is that we get freedom or even the promise of heaven or ultimate harmony, but at the price of some people (especially children) having to endure unspeakable suffering, that is not a satisfactory deal. As Ivan says:

> such harmony is overpriced. We cannot afford to pay so much for a ticket. And so I hasten to return the ticket I've been sent . . . it isn't that I reject God; I am simply returning him most respectfully the ticket that would entitle me to a seat.[1]

True, we don't have to build cities on major fault lines, but does this have to be a world in which tectonic plates rub against one another, creating the devastation of earthquakes and tsunamis? Could there not have been a better world than this? And if human free choice is the problem, what about whole species of animal life that were wiped out long before humans started arguing and throwing spears about?

The free will argument has always struggled to explain what is called 'natural evil' – disease, earthquakes and volcanic eruptions, which don't appear to be caused by human choices. The argument from free will is a hard line to take when faced with childhood leukaemia, rampant cholera or a forest fire that destroys homes and people.

The free will defence makes sense of a lot of our struggles, but doesn't answer all the questions. It's like a piece of a jigsaw, not the whole picture.

The means of maturity

Another set of answers suggests that suffering and evil are a necessary part of working out the great plan for the world, so God has built them in to the system for a purpose. One version of this is the idea that without suffering we would never grow into mature, responsible, thoughtful human beings. The poet John Keats, soon after his brother Tom's death in 1818, and just a few years before his own from tuberculosis at the age of twenty-five, wrote to his brother George: 'Do you not see how necessary a world of pains and troubles is to school an intelligence and make it a soul? A place where the heart must feel and suffer in a thousand diverse ways?' He went on to describe the world as a 'vale of soul-making'. For him, as for the early Christian theologians Irenaeus and Origen and twentieth-century Christian philosopher John Hick, suffering and evil are a necessary part of a world in which we need to grow into maturity. John Calvin offered a not unrelated strand of thought, arguing that God allows bad things to happen to us as part of a larger plan, which we, as finite and limited creatures, do not have the capacity to understand, so we simply have to trust that God knows what he's doing.

There is something to be said for this approach. Our struggles do define and shape us, and how we respond to the challenges that face us in life determines a great deal how we develop as people, whether as bitter, angry souls or as compassionate, healthy ones. Many of the most remarkable and wise people are also those who have been through significant periods of suffering. And many of the shallowest, least reflective people are those who have never had to face anything particularly difficult. Undoubtedly, also, a kind of comfort can be gained from the belief that whatever happens to you, however terrible, is somehow designed by God for your ultimate good.

But there's a big problem. A great deal of suffering in the world in no way leads to moral maturity. How can long-term mental illness with no possible recovery help you grow as a person? Why do some forms of agonizing pain go far beyond what appears necessary for personal growth? Try telling a parent losing a child to leukaemia that this is somehow good for them or for their precious child. This argument actually tries to turn evil into good, saying that somehow it's necessary and good for us. And if it is good for us, why should we resist it? In Albert Camus' novel *The Plague*, when a deadly infectious disease hits a town, the local priest interprets the plague as God's judgement on the people and advises submission to the will of God. It is the atheist local doctor who sees this as a challenge to life and so resists it with all the medical skill and energy he has. The atheist is right. And what about animal suffering? Animals can't mature morally or repent of their sins, so why do they have to suffer?

No doubt some suffering can lead to wisdom and maturity. It fills in another piece of the jigsaw. Yet like the free will argument, it doesn't give an ultimately satisfying answer as to why it has to be this way.

The power of evil

A third set of arguments sees evil not as the fault of human choices or as God teaching us a lesson, but maintains that it comes from an equal and opposite force to God – Satan, the Devil, Lucifer or whatever you want to call it. This argument lets God off the hook for any responsibility for evil, laying the blame firmly and squarely at the feet of an evil power that is working actively against God and all that is good.

Now, there are times when it does seem as if some dark, mysterious power overtakes us. When we do something quite out of character, we occasionally use the phrase 'I don't know what came over me', a hint perhaps that somehow, sometimes, we are influenced to do things by impulses that originate outside ourselves and that we cannot explain. This can happen on a national, corporate level as well. Many Germans in the late 1940s looked back on the Nazi ideology that had consumed the nation over the previous decades and wondered how something so evil could have taken such a firm grip on a modern, rational and mature society such as theirs. Our constant penchant for horror movies and ghost stories, and even our use of the word 'evil' to describe events that seem beyond human comprehension, also signals an awareness of a power that is more than just our own imagination or the effects of our actions, but is somehow bigger and darker than our own hearts.

Yet, like the others, this argument doesn't quite satisfy. In the early Christian centuries, this approach was taken by Manichaeism, a system of thought that for a while attracted the young St Augustine, until he began to realize that, while it had the advantage of removing God's responsibility for evil, it came at a significant cost. If evil is an equal and opposite power to good, if the Devil is the divine counterpoint to God, then God is no longer the ultimate power in the universe. He has a rival. As Augustine recognized, it proves hard to see the point of worshipping a God who cannot really do much about evil in his world, other than wring his hands like a mild-mannered teacher watching a school riot, wishing it would just stop.

Even more important, this just doesn't fit with a Christian understanding of God. Christians have always believed that only goodness is eternal; evil is temporary. If the Devil exists, he is not some kind of equal to God, but a created being, a fallen angel who has turned against God, is now in constant rebellion against him and will one day be consigned to a fiery end. God has no ultimate rivals.

Once again, there is a degree of truth in this attempt to explain evil, which we will come back to later, but such dualism just can't work as a final answer to all the suffering in the world.

Finding a way forward

You can find much more detailed and fine-tuned versions of these arguments, but while there is an element of insight in all of these lines of thinking, none of them quite provides a fail-safe, neat solution, enabling us to file the problem of evil away in a box marked 'problems solved'.

Strangely, to modern ears at least, you can scour the pages of the Bible and never find a neat argument for why there is suffering and evil in God's world. All you get are hints. Yes, human choices do explain a good deal of the suffering in the world, and we can see how our actions have wider, more indirect consequences than we often realize. It is undoubtedly true that the experience of suffering can on occasions be morally beneficial in producing maturity and wisdom. After all, the ironic symbol of Christian faith is a cross, the instrument of torture used to murder the Son of God. Christians wear it proudly because they believe that through the death of Jesus, sins are forgiven and the world is redeemed. Good things, even the best of things, often come through suffering and pain. And yes, sometimes we do find ourselves or others doing things that defy explanation and that make us resort to the language of demonic possession or evil influence. None of these gives a total explanation for the existence of evil, but they are important pieces for constructing a mysterious jigsaw picture that begins to emerge as we put them together.

The power of darkness

There is one more line of thinking that no more provides a total answer than any of the others, but does suggest a reason why it's not easy to make any sense of evil.

A long tradition of thought about evil, with both Greek and Christian roots, sees it not as a positive active principle, a substance, a thing, some kind of opposite force to good, but as the absence of good. It is what Augustine came to in the end after he had found the dualistic tendencies of Manichaeism so unsatisfying. When a tree casts a shadow in my garden, I can talk of the shadow as a thing, just like I talk of the tree as a thing, but, of course, in reality, they are two very different entities. The tree is something substantial and solid – I can feel it, climb it or stub my toe on it. The shadow is not a thing at all; it is the absence of something – the absence of sunshine. Darkness is not really a 'thing', but is merely the absence of light. In the same way, evil is not a 'thing'; it is the absence of Good. It is a no-thing. Grief is the ache left by the absence of a loved friend or partner. Injustice and chaos are the absence of order. Pain is the absence of health. The problem is that in our medically enhanced world we often assume that health is just 'normal' – pain seems far more substantial and noticeable. Imagine it the other way around though – that health is an active gift, something good and *real*. When it goes, all it leaves is the painful process of decay that, unchecked, leads to death and nothingness.

In this way of thinking, all that exists is good. There are no bad things, just good things that have gone wrong. In the book of Genesis, at the end of the initial process of creation, the text says, 'God saw everything that he had made, and indeed, it was very good.'[2] According to this story, the problem of evil and suffering is not due to a fault in creation, like a pot made by an incompetent potter with a small, barely perceivable crack, which in time gets bigger and ultimately makes the pot useless. There is no crack in the original pot, no poison mixed in with the original brew. In the Genesis story, things begin to go wrong not in the first chapter but in the third, when the particular species that was meant to look after it, nurture and care for it (that's us), turns away from the Creator, because it thinks it knows better.

Evil happens when created things like us (or maybe even perhaps mysterious angelic beings before we even got here) turn away from the source of life and love and, instead, turn inwards on themselves. If you can imagine it, it is like a flower deciding to turn away from the sun because it likes the earth it is rooted in better, curving itself back towards the dirt and shrivelling and dying for lack of light and warmth as it does so. It happens when the creation that God made turns away from him, from love, from existence, from light, back towards the darkness and the nothingness from which it was originally summoned. Evil is the impulse that tries to undo or destroy all that God has created.

So when we ask the question as to why evil exists, it isn't really a question that makes sense. Evil does not 'exist' in the sense that God exists or you exist or the lamp post outside my window exists. When we ask why God permits evil or what purpose does it serve, there cannot be an answer – evil has no purpose, because it is the absence of purpose. It can have no meaning, because it is the absence of meaning. It can have no explanation because it is the absence of explanation. It can have no point, because it is by definition pointless.

This is why evil cannot ultimately be explained and why in the final sense there cannot be a neat answer to the problem of evil, because evil is the absence of answers. There is a moment in the Batman film *The Dark Knight* in which the Joker prowls around a huge pile of cash, stolen from the banks of Gotham City, along with various accomplices from the criminal underworld. While the ordinary villains are licking their lips at this enormous heist, the Joker, to their dismay, starts to pour petrol on the bank notes, setting light to the mountain of cash. He then delivers a telling line: 'It's not about money – it's about sending a message: everything burns.'

It's a perceptive insight into the nature of evil. Evil, ultimately, cannot enjoy anything. It cannot create anything; it cannot build anything. It is ultimately about emptiness, about destruction – it simply wants to ruin everything and reduce it to nothing. The petty criminals of Gotham City may have stolen the money, but they never plumb the depths of evil, because they still want to enjoy the fancy watches, the big houses and fast cars that it brings. The Joker alone knows the real significance of evil: that it just annihilates everything. Jealousy fractures relationships, violence kills people, sickness undermines health, infidelity destroys marriages, carbon dioxide emissions devastate our planet.

The Harry Potter novels have a similar understanding of evil. Dementors are ghostly, soul-less beings, who exist purely to suck the life and joy out of other beings, reducing them to nothing but their worst memories. The 'Dementor's kiss' is where they clamp their jaws on a person and suck out his or her soul, as it were. The effect of this chilling encounter with evil is that the victim ends up existing merely as an empty shell, the body lingering on, but the soul evaporating. Evil simply destroys. It leads to absence, emptiness, loss.

Evil happens when goodness vanishes. So to blame God for creating evil alongside good is to make another simple category mistake. No one created evil, because evil is the opposite of creation. It is like a broken chair. You can ask who made the chair, you can even ask who broke it, but you can't ask who made the brokenness, because the brokenness is not a 'thing' like the chair is.

But if evil is the absence of good, if it is essentially nothing, that leaves an obvious question: why does it wreak such havoc? Why does it seem so uncontrollable and cause such pain? St Augustine suggests this response: imagine for a moment going without food or drink for several months. In a sense you are not doing anything – just stopping feeding yourself. A lack of food is just that: a lack, not a 'thing'. But the effects are catastrophic. You will gradually lose weight, shrivel and die if you don't eat or drink for weeks, months on end.

In a sense, evil can do nothing on its own, because it is nothing. It can only do something when it is allowed to possess something that really does exist. Evil is parasitic – it turns good things bad – and the more powerful that thing is, the worse havoc it can wreak. A school bully can make another kid's life miserable; a malicious father can damage a whole family; the leader of a nation can harm a whole population; a technologically proficient human race can, if it chooses, destroy a whole planet. The more powerful a thing is, the more damage it can do when it turns bad.

To go back to Harry Potter, Voldemort, the character who embodies the heart of evil in the books, starts as a disembodied shell, a shadow, a kind of insubstantial vapour, lacking any physical form. He had tried to kill Harry Potter as a child with a curse, but it rebounded on him and the result was that he lost his body, becoming this vague shadowy presence. He longs to recreate his own body, but can only do so by sharing another's body. At this early stage of the story, he is only able to wreak his damage by inhabiting other things, whether the bodies of other characters, such as Tom Riddle or Ginny Weasley, or things such as the 'horcruxes', objects that contain his disembodied self. It is only when he is able to regain his own full body that he can exert his full dark powers again. Without occupying some kind of body, Voldemort is unable to do any real damage at all.

It is a bit like a virus. Viruses are minute bits of genetic material that can only live and multiply inside the cells of other living things. They attach themselves to a host cell, replicating themselves within that originally healthy cell. While sometimes viruses can be beneficial, in the wrong place they can cause infectious disease. When that happens, they are parasitic, as evil always is. In a way, a virus can do no harm until it distorts and twists existing healthy cells into something damaging and destructive – when viruses act like this, they offer a pretty good picture of what evil is and does. Evil on its own can do nothing. It can only worm its way into something good that God has made – whether healthy cells or human minds and souls – and twist them away from their true purpose and goal, turning them in on themselves in a pattern of self-destruction.

This idea of evil as the absence of good adds another important part of the jigsaw. It doesn't give us a nice neat answer to the problem of evil, but it does explain why there might not be one. It isn't that if we were sufficiently intelligent we would understand it – it is that the very nature of evil as the absence of order, goodness and rationality means that it simply can't be explained. Trying to find an explanation for it trivializes it. To rationalize evil is a typically modern strategy – to think that everything can be explained if we think about it hard enough.

What is to be done?

When faced with sheer evil, unutterable pain or meaningless suffering, arguments don't really help much. When you're in pain and there's no easy way to alleviate it, you don't need an explanation as to why this is happening to you; you need someone to stand with you in it, which brings us to the crux of the matter: how you face it.

In the end, all our answers to the mystery of evil can only ever be partial and incomplete. We can get glimpses of an answer, but because evil is ultimately irrational, we can give no reason for it. However, there is another and sometimes more immediate question: what we do about it? We might conclude that these arguments don't work and decide not to believe in God, but by doing that, have we solved the problem of suffering? We still have to deal with it like everybody else. The question is where to find the resources to do that. The most urgent problem of suffering is often how you get through it, not how you explain it. Deciding not to believe in God because it's difficult to reconcile a good God with the existence of evil in the world may provide temporary relief, but it doesn't necessarily help when you get the cancer diagnosis, when you're convicted of something you didn't do or when an economic downturn leads to business failure, bankruptcy and unemployment. You still somehow have to find some hope that failure and fate are not the last word.

I have never met a Christian who claims to have understood and answered the problem of evil. People still believe, despite being fully aware of this potential difficulty to Christian faith. It's not that they don't think about it. There may be some Christians who hardly give it a thought, although I often feel they are the ones most likely to give up on faith when something difficult happens, because they have never really had to face genuine suffering and to hold on to faith in the middle of it. Many Christians over the years, however, have thought long and hard about it and still believe in God nonetheless. When asked the question about whether the Grenfell Tower fire had shaken the faith of people in the local area, I could not recall one conversation that indicated this had happened. North Kensington is a very religious area, with many Christians and Muslims living side by side and, in most cases, the tragedy had made people turn towards their faith, not away from it.

Christians don't believe in God because they have solved the problem of evil. It's just that they have discovered something that stands over against the problem and makes them believe anyway. They have heard the story of a God who gifted us a world that despite the perplexing presence of evil is still an extraordinarily beautiful and joy-giving place. The story goes on to tell of how this God entered into the heart of the very darkness of the world to rescue and redeem it, then invites us to become part of the solution rather than part of the problem by turning us outwards from our self-obsession, teaching us to love again. Over against the enigma of evil, we get the assurance as we are invited to look at the face, the hands, the life, the death and resurrection of Jesus, that God is good after all, that he has conquered evil and will one day eradicate it once and for all. That is why Christians believe. Because it gives them hope.

Atheism may dispense with the difficulty of believing in the goodness of God in the face of suffering, but it comes at a cost. That cost is having to believe that there is no particular purpose behind the apparent randomness of the world, other than the urge for survival. Richard Dawkins writes: 'finally and inevitably, the universe will flatten into a nothingness that mirrors its beginning . . . If you think that's bleak and cheerless, too bad. Reality doesn't owe us comfort.'[3] He may be correct that we have no right to comfort, but it doesn't make it any easier to live without it, especially if we are going through intense pain and loss ourselves. Somehow, in the face of suffering, you have to find hope, because without hope there is just despair and it's very difficult to live life there.

Now, this isn't to prove or disprove Christianity or atheism or anything else. Just because Christianity might give you hope doesn't make it true, any more than the bleakness of some atheist views of the world makes them untrue. It is, however, saying that we need to find the resources to face the struggles of our lives and the pain of the world and hope is essential for doing that. If we need hope to live by, this might just be an indication that real hope, rather than comfortless despair, is possible. C. S. Lewis once wrote this:

A man's physical hunger does not prove that that man will get any bread; he may die of starvation on a raft in the Atlantic. But surely a man's hunger does prove that he comes of a race which repairs its body by eating and inhabits a world where eatable substances exist. In the same way, though I do not believe (I wish I did) that my desire for Paradise proves that I shall enjoy it, I think it a pretty good indication that such a thing exists and that some men will. A man may love a woman and not win her;

but it would be very odd if the phenomenon called "falling in love" occurred in a sexless world.[4]

The same point might be made about love and hope. If we were made to thrive on love and hope, this might be an indication that such things are real and that we should follow the best trail that leads to love and hope wherever that might take us.

To heal a broken world, to build the kind of communities and friendships that can help us cope with the struggle of life, to reverse the damage we are doing to the delicate framework of the natural world, will need a radical change of attitude and behaviour. The world cannot long survive our desire to grab as much as we can for ourselves and to consume its resources for our own personal pleasure. The turn inwards – the heart curved in on itself, as Luther put it – rather than outwards towards our neighbour and the achingly beautiful world we have been given and, beyond that, to the God who gave them both to us, is, it turns out, right at the heart of our modern problems.

All those pouting Instagram posts, the selfies, the constant advice to ignore others and 'be yourself', might they after all not be the path to popularity and success, but signs of the malaise at the heart of modern life? Could it be that this very turn away from God, the rejection of any sense of cosmic order and the resulting focus on ourselves as the only arbiters of truth and identity, is part of our problem?

'All those pouting Instagram posts, the selfies, the constant advice to ignore others and "be yourself", might they after all not be the path to popularity and success, but signs of the malaise at the heart of modern life?'

But if we still find ourselves stuck, turned in on ourselves, either out of greed or hurt, and need to find a way to change, the next chapter looks at how that change might come.

6

Why justice matters and why we don't really want it

A little while ago, a video was doing the rounds on Twitter. It was of a fifteen-year-old boy from a Syrian refugee family in a local British school being held in an armlock, headbutted and kicked by a bigger English boy on the way home from school. The video had gone viral. A quick glance down the list of replies to the original posting revealed an enormous howl of outrage. How could this happen to a quiet boy in a normal school? When you think of all that he and his family had endured, escaping the horrors of Syria for a better life in England, how could he end up at the mercy of an ignorant bully like this?

Of course, this kind of thing happens every day in every town, in every country across the world. When I was at school, there were bullies who picked on smaller, spottier, quieter, more vulnerable kids, and I expect the same was true for you when you were at school or is now if you still are. So why are we outraged? Given that it happens all the time, why don't we just get used to it, shrug our shoulders and simply be grateful that it wasn't us who had a knee in the groin this time?

The fact that we don't points to something significant about human experience. When a person is victimized because of the colour of his or her skin, a crush at a football match kills innocent spectators, a financial crash affects millions of poorer people across the world or a small kid is bullied at school, we sense it's not just that an accident has taken place, but something deeper has gone wrong. A transgression has occurred against some kind of moral law that runs deeper than our own preferences. And when such a transgression takes place, the instinctive cry is for justice for the victims.

The cry for justice is somehow hardwired into us. Every nation on earth has a legal system, built up over many years, entirely focused on seeing that justice happens, those who do wrong are punished and those who have been injured are recompensed. Some of those systems work better than others, and are sometimes sidelined by dictators or coups, but that doesn't silence the cry for justice – if anything, it sounds even louder at those times when it is conspicuously absent.

We may not always be able to agree on what is an offence and what isn't, but this determination to see justice done appears to be a universal human experience, visible wherever you go in the world. Despite the nostalgic laments of an erosion of moral standards, it testifies to a deep sense in all of us that we cannot simply accept it and move on when something goes wrong. The cries of the victims cannot go unheard.

The flaw in the garden

In the last chapter we looked at the flaw at the heart of everything, the evil that stalks our world and the resultant suffering that lies close to the surface in every life, family and society across the planet. Despite the beauty and wonder of this world we live in, something is deeply wrong.

In recent years we have become aware that we are facing one of the gravest challenges to threaten the future of life on this planet: the increasingly undeniable spectre of climate change. A few centuries ago, the Industrial Revolution seemed the answer to the needs of the human race. By using machines powered by the earth's resources of coal, oil and gas, we could make more things more cheaply, transport them further and, in the process, earn more money for those who were quick enough to get in on the act. Now, two hundred years later, we are not so sure it was such a good idea.

Over the past couple of centuries, as we have pumped greenhouse gases such as carbon dioxide, methane and water vapour into the earth's atmosphere, it has progressively trapped solar radiation inside that very atmosphere, gradually heating up the whole planet like a giant oven. Over one million animal and plant species – that is, 1 in 4 of all the species on the planet – are now threatened with extinction. Global sea levels have been rising over the past century and continue to do so at a rate of about one-eighth of an inch per year. In the twenty years between 1980 and 2000, 100 million hectares of tropical forest were lost – that's an area the size of Belgium. Only 13 per cent of the wetlands present on earth in 1700 were still in existence in the year 2000. The entire delicate ecosystem that sustains life on earth is under threat.

During the lockdown that most of the world experienced during the coronavirus pandemic of 2020, we began to glimpse how much we had damaged our world. For the first time in thirty-five years, the Himalayas were visible from a hundred miles away in India as the smog lifted. A professor of Earth Science at Stanford University claimed that the reductions in air pollution in China caused by disruption to industrial activity probably saved twenty times more lives than were lost due to infection with the virus in that country.

If our world is damaged, who is to blame? Most scientists believe that it is our fault. The population of the world has doubled since 1970, the global economy has grown four-fold and international trade has increased ten times over. As a result of our insatiable appetite for exotic food, travel, cheap goods and energy, we have begun to do what seems to be irreparable damage to this beautiful planet that we call our home. Our use and discarding of plastic has increased ten-fold since 1980, leading to vast islands of the stuff floating in the middle of oceans, and water bottles, cartons and carrier bags being washed up on tropical islands that only a decade or so ago were clean and unspoilt. Plastic does not just appear, like apples growing on a tree, but is a result of our desire for cheap and disposable packaging. The rain forests are not disappearing due to earthquakes or random forest fires, but because of cattle ranching in South America and palm oil plantations in South East Asia. Polar bears are threatened with extinction not because they are being wiped out by larger predators, but because of global warming caused at least in part by human activity.

We are used to all this by now. We are also used to the various possible solutions – eat less red meat, go vegetarian, avoid plastic, don't fly and so on. It's not just climate change, though, that's a problem. Every day, children are abused by adults, bearing their suffering silently and unheard; people go hungry while their rulers go shopping; women are hit, belittled or silenced by men; criminals steal the hard-earned property of others and corrupt officials swindle their way to a fortune on the back of those who work for them. Poor eating habits and undisciplined travel cause viruses to spread out of control, killing millions across the world.

Yet a deeper question often remains unspoken: if we are to blame, where is the justice? When someone is guilty, usually we demand that some kind of justice is done to punish those responsible and somehow restore the balance of right and wrong.

Why do we do it?

Why do we do such terrible things to our planet and to each other? Why do bullies target vulnerable kids? Bullies do what they do often because they themselves were bullied, demeaned or belittled as a child and they simply pass on the damage to someone else. When we are damaged inside, emotionally or mentally, it's as if we are handed a hot coal that is agonizing to hold, so we have to pass it on to someone else to avoid the pain. The reason we damage each other is because our own inner selves are damaged.

'The reason we damage each other is because our own inner selves are damaged.'

But does that excuse us? I read some while ago a story of a teenager who had appeared in court accused of rape. As the court case proceeded, his story came out. His mother was an unemployed, drug-addicted prostitute and his father had left him as a child. The young boy often had to watch his mother having sex, injecting cocaine and getting beaten by the many men who came in and out of their house. He had grown up thinking that this is how you treated women, so when his turn came to relate to girls, he only did what he thought was normal. The background might help explain the behaviour, but it doesn't excuse it. There would have been justifiable outrage if the judge had acquitted him on the basis of his bad upbringing. Not everyone with a disadvantaged background turns to crime or abuse, but it's not surprising when people do.

That may be an extreme case, but the same happens on a lesser level to all of us. Our petty sins can usually be explained by some back story – we tell tales to make our friends laugh at other people because deep inside we are insecure and need to find ways to feel good about ourselves. We get angry and lash out at whoever is nearest (and often dearest) because we feel life has been unfair to us and someone deserves to pay. And yet none of these reasons excuses what we do. In a strange paradox, it is not our fault, but we are still responsible. We are caught in a spider's web of iniquity, with the sins of one generation passed on to the next in a grimly inevitable pattern. It's a bit like the scandal of slavery that underlies so many so-called developed nations. Try as we might to hide or ignore it, it won't go away and affects everything, tainting even the present with its grim legacy of pain.

This is what Christian thinkers have called 'original sin' – the idea that our own pride, envy, greed and laziness, our lack of concern for our neighbour and our enemy, is part of a whole web of wrongdoing that stretches back through our friends who mistreated us, our parents who brought us up, to their parents and grandparents, all the way back to some primeval act, a great, seismic crime against the harmony and beauty of the world and the One who made it.

This is the story that the book of Genesis tells. You don't have to believe in a literal Garden of Eden, a literal Adam and Eve or even a talking snake to get the point of the story, the deep truth that it tells about the human condition.

When the species that was meant to care for and look after the world turns in on itself, away from the light towards the darkness; away from the One who made it, gave it the gift of life and a beautiful, delicate, welcoming world to live in; everything starts to unravel. The man and the woman in the tale soon turn against each other in mutual blame and recrimination, just like any arguing couple, and the following chapters are depressingly full of familiar things from our world: murder of the innocent (Cain killing his brother Abel), environmental catastrophe (a flood that devastates the world), international conflict (the Tower of Babel) and much more. The story captures our world exactly.

The divided self

The cry for justice is a noble thing, a fine thing. Yet, like anything else, it can turn bad. We feel the need for justice, that the perpetrators should be punished, and then try to point the finger at those we think are responsible. That, in itself, isn't a bad thing, but hidden in that accusatory spirit is too often the impulse to look for someone or a particular group to blame, not because they are necessarily at fault, but because they are who they are. It is the instinct to divide the world into good people and bad people and, when we do that, 'we' are, of course, part of the 'good' people and the others (fill in the gaps – Jews, immigrants, capitalists, communists, gays, black people and so on) are the ones to blame.

The idea of original sin, however, doesn't let us do that. The Czech writer and politician Václav Havel, reflecting on his experience as a dissident in Stalinist eastern Europe, once wrote that 'the line between good and evil did not run clearly between them and us, but through each person. No one was simply a victim. Everyone was in some measure co-responsible.' That's absolutely right. There are no irredeemably bad people. There are bad actions that deserve punishment, but no purely evil people. There may be some that have turned so far away from goodness and life that it's hard to imagine them ever being turned back towards the light, but if, as Christian faith says, all that God has created is good, then however much a person may have turned away from the light towards the darkness that leads into nothingness, while they are still alive there is something good in there – even if only the continued existence of life itself.

At the same time, this means that there are no totally good people either. Most action movies divide the world into heroes and villains, the good (who usually win) and the bad (who lose). Wayne LaPierre, the Chairman of the National Rifle Association in the USA, once famously said: 'The only thing that stops a bad guy with a gun is a good guy with a gun.' If only it were that easy. The world is not neatly divided between the good and the bad, with or without guns. We are all a bit of both (that's why guns are dangerous, whoever wields them).

'The world is not neatly divided between the good and the bad, with or without guns'

Some, granted, are more one than the other, but all of us share in that odd mixture of compassion and neglect, truth and lies, bravery and cowardice. At times, we are torn between self-love and self-hatred. We are divided selves.

A UK politician was doing a question-and-answer slot for a political website. He was asked a series of questions that demanded quickfire answers. One of them was 'Winston Churchill – hero or villain?' Being of a leftish persuasion, he thought for a brief moment and instinctively replied 'Tonypandy – Villain', referring to Churchill's decision to send in troops to control striking coalminers in South Wales in 1910. Predictably, he came in for a barrage of criticism for this slur on one of Britain's favourite and most revered prime ministers, whose defenders recited Churchill's virtues, especially his part in saving Britain and Europe from the Nazi threat in the Second World War. Yet the problem was not really the answer, it was the question. It was the instinct, so common in our polarized, Twitter-soaked world, to place people entirely on one side or the other of a moral ledger. Was Churchill a hero or a villain? The reality is that at times he was one, at other times the other. Like the rest of us.

When a celebrity posts something that might be interpreted as denigrating someone of another ethnicity, they are instantly labelled as racist. They then usually deny it and say that some of their best friends are black/white/Hispanic/Asian or whatever, equating to the group they have offended. Finding someone who will own up to the label of 'racist', 'homophobic' or 'sexist' is pretty hard. Yet the presence of racism, homophobia and sexism in our society is obvious to everyone who has eyes to see it. That's why it's much more helpful to think of racist or sexist acts or attitudes rather than people. If we're honest, all of us have a small part inside that doesn't understand, trust or appreciate those who are different from us. We are all unconsciously biased in one way or

> 'all of us have a small part inside that doesn't understand, trust or appreciate those who are different from us'

another, and occasionally that bias slips out, but using adjectives like these to define a person, as if that is all they are, doesn't help.

When someone dies, we tend to emphasize their goodness. Yet eulogies often tell only one side of the story. A vicar friend of mine was taking a funeral in an industrial northern town. Having heard a bit about the deceased, his sermon rehearsed some of what this man had achieved and how much he would be missed by his friends and family. On the way out of the crematorium, the man's brother took my friend to one side. 'Let me tell you something,' he said. 'He was a right bastard.' It was a healthy slap of realism in a moment that was in danger of missing the hard truth. The reality is that the man in the coffin was probably, like the rest of us, a bit of both – sorely missed and having done some good, yet at times a pain in the arse. There are people who were made good, but have turned bad, and that is true of all of us to one extent or another. The instinct to divide the world into good people and bad people just doesn't work.

'The instinct to divide the world into good people and bad people just doesn't work.'

If we can't blame whole groups of bad people out there, what about those who damaged us? A person experiencing mental distress, becoming aware of repeated destructive patterns in their lives, is often pointed towards a psychotherapist, who will help them delve into their past and work out how their parents or some other shadowy figure in their childhood, are responsible for their anxieties and neuroses. This process can help explain a lot of what we have become. As the Genesis story tells us, we are caught in a tangled web of evil that goes back a long way, and it can make sense of our inexplicably damaging behaviour to others to understand why we do what we do.

There is real value in this. Abuse or damage committed in the past has to be uncovered and dealt with, justice done and healing found. Yet we miss the point of the story of Adam and Eve if we exonerate ourselves by simply blaming those who came before us. Our human ancestors, whether primeval humans or even our immediate parents or grandparents, may help explain why we have a twist in our nature, a deep insecurity that plays out in the way we treat those closest to us, but it doesn't let us entirely off the hook. They may have passed the hot coal on to us, but, equally, someone handed it to them, and we are responsible for handing it on to the others who we hurt in our turn.

Owning up

I cannot point the finger at anyone else, whether Adam and Eve, my parents, immigrants, criminals or even an annoying neighbour, but I have to start with myself. I cannot begin to answer the problem of evil without recognizing that it starts in my own heart. The line between good and evil runs not

'I cannot point the finger at anyone else . . . I have to start with myself'

between different groups of people, but within every human heart, including my own.

I am part of the cause of climate change. Even if I try to avoid it as much as possible, I am caught up in the system every time I use a plastic bag, eat chocolate, drink coffee or cow's milk, drive my car or fly in a plane. In our globally networked world, where products reach us through a bewildering chain of producers and transit arrangements, it is almost inevitable that somewhere along the line, in the things we consume, someone will have been unfairly treated to enable us to enjoy what we assume is our right to enjoy. I am part of this tangled web of injustice when the clothes I wear or the food I eat was produced by workers in another part of the world who were underpaid for what they did. It is virtually impossible to live in our intricately connected world without some involvement in its injustices. And that is even before I mention my own jealousy of those who succeed where I fail, my grumpiness when things don't go my way, my walking past the homeless man who sits by the station entrance because I'm too busy, the thoughtless words uttered to my family and the whole army of ways in which I add to the pain of the world. If all this is true, I just can't demonize and lay the blame on particular groups, which has been the tendency of the human race ever since it began. The buck stops with me.

There is, however, one distinction that needs to be made. The idea of justice that we have been exploring does make a distinction between the perpetrators and the victims of injustice. Once again, we're all a bit of both, but it's hard to deny that some people in the world are more perpetrators than victims and some victims more than perpetrators. The child who suffers daily, silently, from the abusive, angry father; the workers who are underpaid and then laid off at a whim by companies trying to make as much profit as possible; the victim of rape, left with a life of shame due to no fault of her own – theirs is the real cry for justice. And it is a cry directed both at the offenders, the ones who act unjustly, and at God himself, for making a world where such injustice is possible.

We can ignore this, continue in our unjust ways, consciously or unconsciously fleecing the poor, pillaging the earth, benefiting from the exploitation of others, allowing the malice in our hearts free rein. But God, if he is the originator and upholder of the moral structure of the world, cannot ignore it. Justice must be done for those who receive no justice in this world. Street preachers speak of God's 'wrath', which usually conjures up images of a vengeful bearded deity sitting on his cloud frowning and wondering who to strike with his next thunderbolt. Yet that is a caricature. God's 'wrath' is, in truth, his anger at all the injustice, cruelty and brutality of the world – all that sucks the life out of us and from the beauty of the world he has made. The well-known story in the book of Genesis of the great flood that threatens to wipe out all life on earth has a strangely contemporary ring to it. God looks down on the beauty of the world he has made and at the very centre of it sees us – the very species who were chosen to look after it as it developed, busy destroying it. As he sees the damage we do to his precious creation and to each other, he is filled with regret: 'the LORD was sorry that he had made humankind on the earth, and it grieved him to his heart'.[1] And yet he cannot bring himself to see the whole of humanity vanish, and so he saves Noah and his family to see if they can make a new start. To leave things as they are, to let evil run riot and destroy everything, is not an option. A God who doesn't get angry at injustice isn't worth worshipping.

Selfie anyone?

Now, this isn't to make us all feel bad about ourselves. It is just trying to bring some realism. None of us is all bad. But none of us is all good. And the sooner we own up to this the better. It's why the idolizing of the self so common in our culture is just dishonest. The version of ourselves that we allow to go public on Twitter or Instagram is usually only a half-truth. We post the pictures that make us look good. We delete the ones that make us look fat or bleary-eyed. We present ourselves as caring, thoughtful, funny people and hide the cowardice or envy that is every bit as true of us as the good bits. Telling ourselves or our children that we are amazing, special, unique and lovable is only ever half of the story. Yes, each of us is unique, with huge potential and capacity for goodness. Yet each of us is also flawed, damaged, liable to hurt as well as help, and we just have to be honest with ourselves and each other about it. If we only ever emphasize one side of this puzzle about human nature, we refuse to face up to our complicity in the damage we cause and fly in the face of justice. We also set ourselves or our children up for a fall, when they turn out average in exams, when they don't succeed at what they had set their hearts on

'We need a much more robust basis for building a sense of our own value than telling ourselves that we are simply amazing.'

or when life just turns out to be not the way they expected. We need a much more robust basis for building a sense of our own value than telling ourselves that we are simply amazing.

The French philosopher Blaise Pascal used to say that there are two things you need to grasp about human nature: our *grandeur* and our *misère* – our greatness and our wretchedness. We are made for glory, and sometimes even achieve it, yet we are flawed and damaged, inflicting harm as well as healing. Reflecting on the dignity and the frailty of each human person, he made an astute observation: 'All these examples of wretchedness prove his greatness. It is the wretchedness of a great Lord. The wretchedness of a dispossessed king.'[2]

If you only ever emphasize one of these, you will always misunderstand the complexity of people. However, this is a delicate balance to achieve. Some of us are only too aware of our frailties and need to be told repeatedly that we are carefully and wonderfully made by God, that we have gifts to offer, that we are valued. People who have been deeply damaged by life, which usually means by others, need to hear that loud and clear. Others of us, in contrast, need to face up to those frailties a bit more, recognizing we are not as much God's gift to the world as we thought we were.

If it's true that this world came into being through love, the driving force of the universe, then evil can perhaps best be described as what happens when we start to oppose that force and work against it. Real love starts with a self-forgetful desire for and fascination with the beloved and continues in the ability to sacrifice our own immediate desires, needs or wants for the sake of someone else, a way of life in which we find ourselves most fulfilled. Love is a turning outwards, an opening up, however vulnerable that makes us feel, to God our Maker and to the people he has placed around us. The opposite to love is turning away from it. It is turning away from the God of love who made the world and from the people he has placed around us who need our love to thrive. It is a turning inwards, a turning in on ourselves. The opposite of love is not hatred but indifference. It is being and becoming indifferent to God or to the needs and desires of

'The opposite of love is not hatred but indifference.'

my neighbour, because I am more interested in my own fortunes. Bigging ourselves up may seem like the answer to low self-esteem, but actually it turns out to be part of the problem.

Evil happens when people get so wrapped up in themselves that they become isolated within a self-enclosed, self-centred bubble, in which they turn inwards, wither and die, neglecting their neighbours or turning against them in

'Bigging ourselves up may seem like the answer to low self-esteem, but actually it turns out to be part of the problem.'

hatred, like a virus that turns bad and destroys everything it touches and finally even itself, so that there is nothing – literally nothing – left.

Yet so many aspects of our culture seem to encourage us to focus our attention on ourselves. In order to sell us things, it tries to get us to think constantly about what we look like and how we can make ourselves look good so that others like us a bit better. It preys on our insecurities and anxieties and is very good at it. Our habit of being preoccupied with ourselves is the very thing that underlies so much of the wrong in the world. Finding redemption requires that somehow we need to be turned outwards, becoming less self-obsessed. Imagine losing that crippling anxiety about how other people see us, that fear of missing out, the worry over whether people will really find out what we have done or thought?

Towards the end of Will Storr's book, he writes this:

One of the dictums that defines our culture is that we can be anything we want to be . . . We just have to dream, to put our minds to it, to want it badly enough . . . We internalise it, incorporating it into our sense of self. But it's not true. It is, in fact, the dark lie at the heart of the age of perfectionism. It's the cause, I believe, of an incalculable quotient of misery. Here's the truth that no million-selling self-help book, famous motivational speaker, happiness guru or blockbusting Hollywood screenwriter seems to want you to know. You're limited, imperfect. And there's nothing you can do about it.[3]

He's mostly right. The narcissistic age that encourages us to find ourselves and then to be ourselves only leads to insecure, anxious people, never quite sure that they match up to what they think others think they should be. But is there really nothing we can do about it?

We can learn to love. And that is what Christianity is all about. Yet learning to love is no simple matter. Old habits die hard. Something more radical has to happen in us before we can begin to make progress. And that's what the next chapter will explore.

7

Why everyone needs an identity crisis

The last two chapters have taken us deep into the darkness. They have tried to understand the flaw at the heart of everything, the nature of evil and where it comes from. Evil might be best explained as the absence of goodness, and the instinct for justice might make us face up to our part in the injustice of the world, but that doesn't help us much if that is the last word.

All those nature programmes narrated by David Attenborough tell us the story almost as well as the Bible does. This is an astonishingly beautiful world. Blue oceans with bustling coral reefs, rain forests alive with colour and sound, mountains stark and fiercely forbidding. Yet there is a wound at the heart of it. There is the strange mystery of disease and sickness, operating like a virus seeking to destroy life from within. Then there is the even more inexplicable fact that the world is now threatened with destruction, strangled by the very creatures who were supposed to care for it.

And the same story could be told about every human life. We are capable of acts of ordinary and extraordinary kindness – a parent giving up sleep and independence to care for a child; a neighbour opening their home to a refugee; a prisoner voluntarily going to the firing squad to save the rest of his comrades. Yet we are also capable of shocking evil – the father beating his child out of anger; the community that closes its doors to people who desperately need help but who would inconvenience their comfort; the dictator who orders the random prisoner to be executed to teach the others a lesson. However, the cries of the victims of evil in our world won't stay silent. The beaten child, the abandoned refugee, the persecuted prisoner – they are the tip of the iceberg and, try as we might, we cannot shut out their cry for justice.

This is a world of astonishing beauty and unspeakable evil. It can amaze and appal in equal measure. The two are not somehow equal and opposite. The beauty and the goodness somehow belong – they are meant to be there. The horror and the malice are an aberration, an interruption. Which is why the image of a wound works. A wounded leg is a damaged leg, a leg that ought to be fine, but has been cut. Yet this wound goes deeper, right to the heart of the world you and I live in every day. We know wounds can be healed. The big question is whether this one can.

It is not that good and evil have always been mixed together and always will. If that were the case, it would be hard to have much hope that things will ever be any different from what we experience now, which is especially bad news if you are the victim of injustice or cruelty. If evil doesn't belong here, there is the possibility that one day it might be put back in its box and done away with for good. Christianity says that, one day, evil will be defeated. Goodness will triumph. Throughout the Bible we get hints of this, but its final book, the book of Revelation, contains some of the most moving and poetic statements of this hope, one that has sustained countless people who have faced trouble, persecution or injustice over the years:

> See, the home of God is among mortals.
> He will dwell with them;
> they will be his peoples,
> and God himself will be with them;
> he will wipe every tear from their eyes.
> Death will be no more;
> mourning and crying and pain will be no more . . .[1]

In the end, we are promised, Love wins and Evil loses. Every now and again we see it happen right before our eyes. When a wall that has separated families and friends falls, when a notorious paedophile is jailed, when a friend resists the temptation to join in the gossip and stands up for you instead – we see echoes of the triumph of goodness over evil. But then at other times we see the reverse. When a violent gang gets away (literally) with murder, when a child is silently abused over many years with no apparent way of escape, when a young woman commits suicide, unable to stand any longer the long battle with depression, it seems that the darkness triumphs. And at the end of every life, death awaits. It seems that, for all our frenetic activity, death will get us in the end, and there will just be silence.

But what if it is true that the Maker of all things, rather than watching from a distance as his world is trashed, his beloved creatures are wiped out and the people he made destroy each other, entered into the very heart of darkness to redeem and transform it? What if God not only took on human life and lived out the love that has always been in his heart but also went even further, to the lowest point of all, into the worst experience of injustice and abandonment? What if the great healer applied the cure to the very source of the disease? What if one day, death, mourning, crying and pain will be a thing of the past, because in the new world that God promises will one day come about, they won't belong, banished to the dustbin of hell where they came from?

Love and death

When Love enters a world in which evil is rampant, it is bound to lead to trouble. That old self-destruct button, the instinct to turn inwards, always near at hand for the human race, was not a problem for Jesus, because in him we see love made perfect. But it was definitely there in those around him, not just in his enemies, but even in his friends, who at various times abandoned, denied or betrayed him.

His was a life of self-giving, which culminated in the supreme act of self-sacrifice, voluntarily submitting himself to execution on a Roman cross. Jesus could easily have avoided it. One of the strangest parts of the story told in the Gospels is Jesus' refusal to defend himself during his trial. He had numerous opportunities to give his side of the story, to try to secure an acquittal, but time and time again, when asked to explain himself, he just remained silent. He seemed to know that this was the battle he had to fight. He had to enter into the realm of darkness, to face down the power that wanted once and for all to extinguish the light, to destroy Love. When he was finally arrested, he recognized this was what had to happen: 'this is your hour – when darkness reigns'.[2]

So Jesus is arrested and put on trial. It's obvious it is rigged. Even the arrest is shady, with one of his followers bribed to hand him over. At the trial no hard evidence is brought forward that he has done anything wrong, just a few fake witnesses who were happy to misquote him – enough to secure a guilty verdict. Torture follows, leather whips biting into his skin, a mock 'crown' made out of hard, sharp, inch-long thorns pressed into his skull. He is stripped naked for maximum shame. Long, rough nails are driven into his hands and ankles and his battered body is strung up – a deterrent to anyone who dares to oppose the might of Rome. And so he dies. Not quietly in his bed like most people, but enduring one of the most horrific forms of death imaginable, sharing the fate of many over the centuries whose lives have ended in squalor and agony.

Yet it was even worse than that. Suffering can be bearable if you feel that someone stands with you and you are not alone. Many religious people have been able to endure torture and martyrdom through the belief that God is with them. Yet on that grim Friday outside the walls of Jerusalem, Jesus doesn't even have that. Hanging there, abandoned by his supposed followers who fled at the first sign of trouble, his closest friend even pretending that he had never heard of him, he can't even find the comfort of the presence of God his Father – a presence he had felt throughout his life and that was the secret of his own security and peace. At this vital moment, even that deserts him, as he groans, 'My God, why have you forsaken me?'[3] The name he uses is significant. Usually he had called God 'Abba' – the intimate Aramaic word for a Father. Now he uses the more distant word 'Eloi' – his Father had disappeared behind a cold veil of silence. If heaven is the place where God and goodness are fully present, hell is the place where he is totally absent. Jesus ventures into hell itself, entering the very stronghold of evil.

If that had been the end of the story, it would mean there is no ultimate answer to injustice and, most chillingly, to death – that it swallows everything. Life, love and even God vanish into its jaws at the end.

Yet it isn't the end. Jesus' bruised, bloodied, pale, dead body is taken down from the cross. The custom was to lay the body out, pack spices around it to stem the smell of decaying flesh, put it in a temporary chamber in a hillside tomb (not buried in the ground), and wait for the flesh to decay until the bones could be gathered and finally placed in a small brick box to be stashed away for good. Jesus' body never got that far. A couple of days after his execution, stories began to circulate that he had been seen alive again. It started with one of his closest followers, Mary, claiming she had met him in the garden nearby, after she had found no trace of the body in the tomb. There was another appearance before his friends in the familiar room where Jesus used to meet with them, an encounter with a couple on a longish walk to a nearby village, then numerous other similar stories back up in Galilee where it had all begun.

Just to be clear, this was not resuscitation. It was no flashy miracle, showing that God can bring dead people back to life. Jesus did that at least twice, to the son of a grieving widow in a village called Nain and to a friend of his called Lazarus, but both of them presumably lived for some time afterwards, only to then die again, this time for good. Jesus' resurrection is different: this is not coming back from the dead, but passing through death and reappearing on the other side – the only time it has ever happened. There are no analogies to it. The main objection to it over the years – that dead people just don't rise and that nothing like it has ever happened before – misses the point. This was not an event that follows the pattern of other events. It was by definition unique. It was the 'abolition of death', as one of the early Christians put it.[4] If this were true, it would change everything.

Of course, it's hard to believe. But before dismissing it as a legend dreamt up by unsophisticated pre-modern people, bear in mind a few things. People back then were not stupid. They knew as well as we do that dead people don't suddenly come alive again. Yes, there are stories of dying and rising gods or even of dead ancestors appearing again to their descendants, but not stories of a man appearing alive who died just two days ago – claims that could easily be disproved by producing the body. And whatever happened, those closest to the event, those who presumably would have known it was a sham if it had been, were so convinced it was true they spent the rest of their lives speaking about what happened that weekend, some of them even being executed for it. As the comedian Milton Jones put it: 'if the resurrection was fake you have to say the scam has gone miraculously well'.

All right – none of this is proof. But then you don't have to have absolute proof to believe. Many of the most important things we believe – that our parents really were our parents, that we will live through this day, that our closest friends love us – we believe without absolute proof, because it seems to make sense and offers a much better way to live if it is true. You can't believe in something that is obviously a fake, but just for a moment, imagine that it did happen – for once in the history of humankind, God, who after all is the Creator and therefore presumably can do this kind of thing, did raise someone from the dead? And not just someone – a man who lived a life of utter and complete love, yet who had been unjustly convicted, tortured and beaten savagely, subjected to one of the most horrific and painful deaths ever devised?

Victims and villains

If this did happen, what does it mean for us? The brutal death and unexpected resurrection of Jesus has been interpreted in a whole host of ways over the years. The New Testament itself uses a number of pictures to describe what happened – it is like a ransom paid to free a captive, a sacrifice offered to take away offences, a fine paid so a debtor can go free. Yet underneath there is the conviction that in this series of events over that one weekend two thousand years ago, the world shifted. Decisively. Something changed in history and a new world was born. It's like what happens at the winter solstice in the northern hemisphere every year. As the year heads into autumn, the world heads into the darkness of winter, every day getting shorter and shorter. On 21 December, however, something imperceptible shifts. The earth tilts and the days suddenly start getting longer as summer is on the horizon. It doesn't immediately feel any different. The following day – 22 December – usually feels much like 21 December: cold, wet and cloudy. Yet something really has changed. Likewise, the world can still feel full of darkness and the icy winds of injustice. Yet, because of that one weekend in Jerusalem two thousand years ago, something in the world has dramatically moved.

We continue, though, to experience the dark days of winter even as spring is coming. We still experience for a time the symptoms of the disease even if the underlying infection has been healed. When we look at the injustices of our world, there are always two sides to them. On one side there are the perpetrators, those who commit or benefit from the exploitation of workers, the drug trade, the trafficking of people as slaves across continents. Then there are the victims – the underpaid workers, the addicts, people sold as assets with no regard for their dignity as human beings. But as we saw in the last chapter, it's never quite as simple as that – there is a bit of both in all of us. There is Sin and there is Suffering. They are related but different.

When Jesus, the Son of God, submits to death on a Roman cross, God becomes one of the victims. The Creator of the universe becomes an innocent prisoner sentenced by a miscarriage of justice, convicted by a sham trial. He becomes another victim of human trafficking as he is handed from one weak politician to another, none of them willing to do the right thing and let him go. He is a victim of torture as he is tied to a post and whipped to within an inch of his life. He identifies with those murdered by knife crime as a soldier stabs him in the side with a spear. Even more, he stands alongside every victim who feels abandoned and deserted as he dies alone. It is hard to begin to imagine the desolation in that most agonizing cry in human history – 'My God, my God, why have you forsaken me?' – when Jesus the Son of God experiences the absence of God. The worst kind of suffering is solitary suffering, where bitter tears are shed and no one hears, no one knows, not even God appears to notice. And this is what Jesus goes through on the cross – in a strange, barely conceivable way, God experiences the absence of God. On the cross, Jesus stands in our place when we are in the worst place of all.

Yet, despite this experience of abandonment, he is not forgotten. God does see, God does remember and, before long, God does the most astonishing thing: he raises Jesus from death, breaking the one great barrier that ends all life, opening a crack in the dark wall that approaches every one of us as we approach the end of our lives. The love that empowered Jesus throughout his life, the love that brought Lazarus back from his grave, that restored the sight of a blind man, that healed a woman with severe internal bleeding that made her ritually unclean so unable to touch anyone for years – that love was so strong that not even death was a match for it.

What does this mean for the victims of this world? *What if it were true that there is nothing we can suffer that puts us beyond the reach of the love of God?* If God himself, in the person of Jesus, went through not only intense physical pain, but also the worse pain of abandonment, not only by his friends but even the absence of God himself, then there is nothing we can experience that is beyond his power to change. Because he experienced the absence of God, we ultimately do not have to. When we feel nothing, when God seems silent, when we doubt whether he even exists, then we look back to Jesus' cross and remember what happened two days later, the demonstration once and for all that God does remember, does see, never abandons, however much we feel he has.

God sides with the victims of injustice, not the perpetrators of it. On that first Good Friday he hung alongside those crucified, not those who delivered their random 'justice'. The resurrection takes this a step further. God did not raise Caesar, Pontius Pilate or the High Priest from their deaths – he raised Jesus, the victim, the one who had suffered at the hands of injustice. This means that those who still suffer at the hands of injustice can also expect vindication one day. Even when justice is not done in this world, there will come a day when the innocence of the victims will be seen, mistaken 'justice' will be reversed and a verdict will be passed on those who caused such evil.

What does this say to the perpetrators of evil? Jesus dies as one of the victims, but there is still something more. As Jesus hangs on the cross, as he looks on the impassive faces of the soldiers who dragged him to this spot, the very ones who drove in the nails, just doing their job, he says: 'Father, forgive them, for they do not know what they are doing.'[5] When Jesus, returning from the other side of death, meets with his friends again, those who deserted him and denied they ever knew him, he says four simple but unbelievably healing words: 'Peace be with you.'[6]

In neither case is there a word of recrimination or blame, just words of peace, reconciliation, forgiveness. As we saw in the last chapter, we do dreadful things to others, at least in part because other people have done dreadful things to us. We hurt others because we are hurting ourselves. Not that this lets us off the hook. But Jesus on the cross soaks up all the anger, the fury, the evil of the world. He takes the worst we can do to him and to all the victims of the world since time began and, rather than returning it with interest, he absorbs it, and through the power of the divine love that pulses through his soul, offers in return only forgiveness and grace. He is handed the hot coal of pain and suffering and, for the one and only time, does not hand it on to someone else to hold, but bears the agonizing pain himself, holds it until it cools and then lets it drop to the ground, empty and harmless. To put it simply: *There is nothing we can do that puts us beyond the reach of the forgiveness of God.*

Even more than this – for both victims and villains (or the victim and villain in all of us) it says that death is not the end. If dying was not the end for Jesus, then death need not be the end for us. Maybe those small hints we get of a life beyond this one, stories of people who are clinically dead but experience something beyond, have a point. A recent article put it this way: 'Though details and descriptions vary across cultures, the overall tenor of the experience is remarkably similar . . . many of these stories relate the sensation of floating up and viewing the scene around one's unconscious body; spending time in a beautiful, otherworldly realm; meeting spiritual beings (some call them angels) and a loving presence that some call God.'[7] Maybe these experiences are small hints of the greatest miracle of all – the Resurrection of Jesus that means the possibility of life beyond this one for each of us.

The decisive victory

The death and resurrection of Jesus speaks to both the villain and the victim in all of us – the parts where we have sinned and the parts where we have been sinned against; the parts where we are the perpetrators of evil and the parts where we are its victims. There is nothing we can suffer that puts us beyond the reach of the love of God, and there is nothing we can do that puts us beyond the reach of the forgiveness of God.

'There is nothing we can suffer that puts us beyond the reach of the love of God, and there is nothing we can do that puts us beyond the reach of the forgiveness of God.'

When St Paul wrote about the death and resurrection of Jesus, he said something remarkable. He said that when that happened, a decisive victory was won over all that held the human race in captivity. It's as if, behind the ideologies, memes and mental maps that we all hold, he sees other powers at work, systems and dim forces shaping us and of which we are hardly aware, making us think and act in the ways that we do. He called them the *stoicheia*: notoriously hard to translate, but sometimes called the 'elemental spirits of the universe'. When Jesus, the Son of God, the Creator in human flesh, stormed the strongholds of death itself, took it on in a cataclysmic battle and won, somehow the human race was released from these 'elemental spirits' of the world.

In Paul's first-century context, these *stoicheia* were found at work in things like (for his own people) strict obedience to the Jewish Law. The idea that the power of the *stoicheia* was broken now meant that Gentiles could access the intimacy of Israel's relationship with God, so anyone could enjoy this without having to become ethnically Jewish. Or (for pagans) it worked through the power of the Greek or Roman gods, who were usually unpredictable and often angry. Because their power was now broken, people were freed from that kind of worship to orientate their lives around the one behind the 'gods' – the One who created all things. The message was that because Jesus has taken on the 'powers' and defeated them, they no longer have any hold over you – you don't have to obey the Jewish Law or the pagan gods, but a different, more liberating kind of law.

If he were here today, I suspect Paul would identify other ways in which these 'elemental spirits' show up. There is the law that says you are only OK if you are thin, beautiful and wear the best clothes. There is the law that says you are OK if you have a large following on social media, become famous and are recognized in the street. There is the law that says you are an autonomous individual, left on your own to design your life and identity, competing with everyone else for a share of wealth, success and fame. There is the law that says you are what you feel, so you have to obey every passing whim or desire, because they are what define you.

The problem is that all of us – victims and villains, in other words; each one of us who is a bit of both – are caught in this same system, under the same power, bound to run along the same railway tracks, follow the same rules. We all end up being competitive individuals, caught in the consumerist race to acquire more money so we can buy more things to feel better about ourselves – a race that is eating away at our souls and corroding the planet on which we live and depend. We are stuck with being autonomous individuals, increasingly isolated from each other and wondering why we feel so lonely.

The message of the cross and resurrection is that YOU DON'T HAVE TO OBEY THESE LAWS. It's not that you don't have to obey any laws at all, but you don't have to obey these limiting, enslaving ones. The cross and resurrection mean that the true 'law' you have to obey is the law of love – the law that offers a way to give up the competitive race to get what you want and instead to think first about what your neighbour needs. It is not the freedom to do what you want; it is the freedom NOT to do what you want, when so often the desires that rise up from the deepest darkest places of our hearts will destroy us, our relationships and our planet.

'It is not the freedom to do what you want; it is the freedom NOT to do what you want'

Identity crisis

When St Paul pondered the meaning of all this, he offered a dramatic way of understanding what it meant. He said: 'If anyone is in Christ, they are a new creation.'[8] To become a follower of Christ was not just a lifestyle choice, adding an extra activity to a busy schedule, such as enrolling for a yoga class or becoming vegan – it was like becoming an entirely new person. It was as if the old 'self', that self torn between self-love and self-hatred, the anxious self, trying to prove itself by getting everyone to like it, was buried with Christ in the tomb and a new self came to life as it was resurrected along with him.

When Paul tried to explain this to early Christian groups, he would talk about two selves: 'your old self, which is being corrupted by its deceitful desires': and 'your new self, created to be like God in true righteousness and holiness'.[9] The trick was to learn to say no to that 'old self'. That is the competitive individual in me that constantly wants attention, is always checking how many followers or likes I get, wants to get its own way, wants everyone to think I am better than everyone else, that gets upset and full of self-pity if I don't get what I think I deserve. It's the self that is happy to help others as long as I don't miss out. It means recognizing that voice in my head, that self, and being quite ruthless with it. It means doing what Jesus says: denying that self.

It also means cultivating our new selves, the new kind of person that is slowly emerging. It means feeding it, nurturing it, encouraging it to grow by learning the rules of this new way of living.

The truth is:

YOU ARE NOT WHAT YOU FEEL
YOU ARE NOT WHAT YOU WEAR
YOU ARE NOT WHAT YOU BUY
YOU ARE NOT WHAT OTHERS THINK YOU ARE
You are instead a beloved child of God, made out of love and made for love

Everything else is working out what that means. This is your new self. From this point onwards, the choices you make are all about encouraging and feeding that new self. This is a self that gains its identity first and foremost not

'This is your new self'

by what we have suffered or the mistakes we have made, the harm we have done, the things we buy or the way others see us, but by the fact that Christ loved us and gave himself for us so that those hurts – both those endured and committed – might be overcome. This is a new self, born out of love and made for a radical reorientation around the love that drives the world towards its future. It is living as if it is true that Jesus is risen, that death and the powers that diminish and will destroy you have been defeated.

This doesn't mean neglecting our own health and well-being (and there are those who especially need to hear this, those who may have a natural tendency to doubt themselves). There is a proper kind of self-love, which means proper care for your body and soul. We are no use to anyone if we neglect our health, don't get proper rest and refreshment and fail to ensure that we look after our own body and soul. When Jesus says, 'love your neighbour as yourself', he assumes that we will make sure we have enough to eat, sufficient clothes to wear, get to do some of the things that give us life and don't indulge in too many of the things that drain us of energy. It's just that he says we should also learn to do the same for our neighbours and even our enemies as well.

So this needs wisdom. And it needs discipline. When children have tantrums because they don't get what they want, good parents will discipline their children to help them learn to discipline their own selfish instincts in time. The problem is, that childish selfishness doesn't go away – we just get better at hiding it, more sophisticated in our ways of making sure we are the centre of attention. There is something in us adults that needs disciplining too.

We need to learn to become skilled at recognizing that voice when it rises in our hearts and being tough with it, learning the wisdom to know the difference between our true, God-given, new Christian self that needs to be nurtured and developed, and that other, old, whiny, self-centred self.

If you want to be a great athlete, you will need to be ruthless on that voice that wants the extra portion of dessert, to stay in bed rather than go training. If you want to pass exams, you need to learn to be hard on the voice inside you that wants to watch TV rather than go and revise. Exactly the same is true of the spiritual life.

The novelist Bruce Chatwin once said, 'if the world has a future, it has an ascetic future'.[10] The world cannot survive our self-indulgence.

> '**Unless we learn to deny our consumptive, greedy, look-at-me selves, we will not only destroy ourselves, but we will destroy our planet as well.**'

Unless we learn to deny our consumptive, greedy, look-at-me selves, we will not only destroy ourselves, but we will destroy our planet as well.

For Paul, it literally meant a new name. Up to this point he had been Saul, but he soon took a new name to indicate his new self: Paul. When babies are born, they inherit a surname from their parents, and are also given their own personal name – Naomi or Noah or Nicholas. Traditionally, this first name was given when a child was baptized – they were given a 'Christian' name – a name that marked them out as a distinct new person from the rest of their family, initiated into this Christian life at an early age, set on the path of following Christ. The task of the Christian is to live out of this new identity, this new Christian self.

Occasionally, people who have been witnesses to a crime or juvenile offenders who are later released to try to start again cannot stay as they are. If they did, they would soon be the target of old enemies or people with a lasting grudge. Such people are sometimes given new identities – a new name, address, passport, wardrobe and the rest. Living with a new identity, however, is not easy. A consultant forensic psychiatrist, asked about the difficulty such people experience, said: 'Double lives are a burden for people. Juggling two identities is stressful and the secrecy takes its toll. People are not necessarily well equipped to do this sort of thing; it's not their natural state.' It's hard living out a new identity, trying to live this new life while the old one still lurks around. Such people often feel a compulsion to go back and live secretly out of their old existence, not who they are now freed to be.

That offers an illustration of what St Paul meant. To follow the way of Jesus is paradoxically to leave behind that old self, the one you were afraid others would see, the one wrapped up in itself, forever anxious about the judgement of other people. It is to welcome a new self, 'created in Christ Jesus for good works, which God prepared beforehand to be our way of life'.[11]

Yet for this to be true for us, both of the perspectives we saw earlier need to be believed. If we don't believe that God stands with us when we are the victim, he cannot help us. Likewise, if we refuse to trust the offer of forgiveness for all the harm we have done or if we try to accept it while continuing in the injustice, we turn it into cheap grace that is not grace at all.

We can, if we choose, receive into the deepest recesses of our hearts that word of Jesus addressed to you and to me as much as those gathered around the rough, dirty cross on the first Good Friday: 'Father forgive them, for they do not know what they are doing.'[12] We can allow that word to rest there and allow it to change our attitudes and our actions. We can hear his voice telling us that he has been where we stood and maybe still stand, that nothing we experience is foreign to the God who made us and we can let that reality slowly heal our damaged souls.

This is ultimately the Christian answer to the problem of evil. It is the appearance of God himself in human form, entering into the very heart of darkness itself, to take on the evil powers and rescue the world from the destructive forces that have invaded it. It's why Jesus spends his time not discussing the problem of evil, but healing the sick, raising the dead, forgiving the guilty, touching lepers.

It's why he chooses to storm the gates of hell and defeat it once and for all.

When God takes on evil, there can only be one winner. Sometimes we hear people say that 'life is stronger than death' or 'love is stronger than the grave'. Observably, this doesn't make any sense at all. One day both your earthly life and mine will, to all intents and purposes, be snuffed out by death. Whatever love we have for our families and friends will apparently come to an end with our, or their, final moments. Death seems to bring an end to all life and love. Christians, however, can say that life and love are stronger than death, because when God took on death in the person of Jesus, death lost. Jesus was raised from death, so that people who hear and believe the promise of vindication and forgiveness can hope that they too, when they face death, will be able to pass through to an even greater life on the other side. Those who put their trust in Jesus, who join themselves to him, as it were, in baptism (St Paul describes how getting baptized is like dying with Jesus as we go under the water and rising with him as we come out) will die like everyone else. Yet the possibility, the promise, is that that moment of death will, in fact, be a gateway into something much richer and greater, the fulfilment of all our best hopes and longings in this life, leaving behind the desires that destroy and, instead, enjoying the very presence of the God who made us.

By dying in the way he did, and passing through death to the other side and back again, Jesus has brought both justice and forgiveness within reach. The love that made the world has defeated the powers ranged against it. We often feel we need to change the world. Christianity relieves us of that burden because it says that the world has already been changed. We live in a world where the power of death and therefore all its grisly allies – suffering, injustice and misery – have been beaten. Our task is not to change the world but to learn to live as if it really has been changed, that we are forgiven our part in its pain, that our Creator stands with us in our struggles. Our task is to live in the joyful relief of knowing that the spring is coming and, after that, the summer – so, one day, the darkness will be conquered and evil will be banished for good.

8

Why freedom is not what you think it is

So what are these new selves to be like? If the powers of darkness have been defeated, how does all this play out in ordinary human lives? Jesus promises at several points that he sets people free, yet if you know anything about Christianity, you'll know it involves some kind of obedience to the will of God, submitting to discipline, giving up things. That doesn't sound a lot like freedom. Or at least it doesn't sound like the kind of freedom we usually have in mind.[1]

You can tell what a culture values by what it goes to war over. In the seventeenth century, we fought our wars over religion. In the nineteenth century, we fought them to build empires. In the twentieth and twenty-first centuries, we fight our wars over freedom. The Second World War was a fight for freedom from Nazi tyranny. The so-called Global War on Terror, announced by President George W. Bush after the attacks of 9/11 was entitled 'Operation Enduring Freedom'. It heralded a series of conflicts in which Western governments, and the USA in particular, sought to export ideas of democracy and freedom to other parts of the world. We can now see that it didn't go quite as planned.

Freedom is one of the big ideas of our culture. Sitting at a desk at work, the trainee solicitor dreams of the freedom to travel or of just sitting on a beach sipping a piña colada. Stuck in a difficult marriage, a wife dreams of being free to find someone else rather than the husband she is stuck with. Working under a vindictive manager, a supermarket stacker dreams of the freedom to start his own business.

Not all that promises freedom actually delivers. When email began to be widely used in the 1980s, the promise was of freedom. No longer would you have to write a letter on paper, put it in an envelope, stamp it, put it in the letter-box and wait for a reply a week or two later (if you were lucky). You could simply type a message, send it instantly and receive a reply straight away. I remember wondering what we were going to do with all the free time we had left over once email arrived.

The mobile phone was the same. No longer would you need to wait in to take a phone call – you could receive and make calls anywhere. The result would be liberation from being tied to home or the need to find a phone box. I don't suppose there are many people who feel liberated by either email or their mobile phones.

The roots of freedom

Freedom became a particularly attractive idea as Europe emerged into the modern period with the desire to be free from the domineering influence of older institutions such as unaccountable monarchies, governments and the Church. The contemporary idea of freedom, as most of us understand it is, in fact, a fairly modern invention, built by a number of key thinkers and activists in the fairly recent past.

One of these was an English country landowner who ended up as the Commissioner of Trade in London, John Locke (1632–1704). For him, the basic unit of society was the individual and, in our original 'state of nature', each individual human being was free and equal. However, that freedom had to be curtailed because there were other people who were also free and equal. So in an exchange that became known as the 'Social Contract', each person traded their absolute freedom to do what they want for submission to the authority of governments. These exist to safeguard the rights of the individual to

'Life, Liberty and Estate', yet they also police the boundaries of our own liberties so that we do not encroach on the interests and preferences of others. The state keeps the peace between us, ensuring each of us can pursue our own chosen path in peace, while ensuring that we don't tread on the toes, or dreams, of others. This is 'the liberty to follow my own will in all things, where the Rule prescribes not, and not to be subject to the inconstant, unknown, arbitrary will of another man'.[2]

The second architect of modern ideas of freedom was an eccentric and introverted Genevan, Jean-Jacques Rousseau (1712–1778). His most remembered phrase was 'Man was born free, but everywhere is found in chains.' He wasn't as optimistic about the effects of government as Locke. For Rousseau, the expectations of societies and governments place limits on the individual, cramping his (and he did largely think in male terms) style. Marriage was a plot to subjugate men, and the ownership of land, for example, was a source of endless injustice, strife and jealousy. His answer to this was not nostalgia for a golden past age but education. Children should be educated to be free. Geography, for example, was to be taught not from books, but by letting children roam free, get lost and find their own way home. Freedom is found by casting off the expectations and traditions of the past, the shackles of custom:

> Nature provides for the child's growth in her own fashion, and this should never be thwarted. Do not make him sit still when he wants to run about, nor run when he wants to be quiet. If we did not spoil our children's wills by our blunders their desires would be free from caprice. Let them run, jump, and shout to their heart's content.[3]

By the way, if you are wondering if Rousseau ever tried to look after a toddler, he actually had five children, packed each one them off to the foundling hospital at birth and promptly forgot about them.

As one writer put it acidly: 'he knew somehow that children would overtax his limited ability for reciprocal affection'.[4]

A third key figure in the development of our modern ideas on freedom was the child prodigy and later colonial administrator in Victorian London, John Stuart Mill (1806–1873). Inspired by the Victorian ideal of progress, Mill believed that the engine of innovation and energy in any society is freedom of expression. People should be free to express their own ideas and opinions, even if they are the only one to hold those opinions. 'Liberty consists in doing what one desires', he said, giving pride of place to the wants and longings that happen to arise in a person's heart. People should also be free to pursue whatever path of life they choose, and express their own unique individuality in whatever way seems right to them. It all came with one caveat. Like Locke – aware that if each of us did exactly what we wanted to, we would end up in conflict and, occasionally, doing what we want might actually end up harming ourselves – Mill argues that there is one, and only one, reason that would justify interfering with another's freedom: when they are about to harm themselves, or others, by their actions.

These three philosophers are among the key architects of the understanding of freedom that most of us take for granted. The key to happiness is freedom. And freedom is my own personal space where I am free to do as I wish, protected by the state, which safeguards those rights and freedoms (Locke); it is the freedom of the natural condition, free of the complexities of cultural expectations (Rousseau); it is freedom of expression, freedom of speech and the opportunity to say and do what I like as long as I don't harm anyone else (Mill). The way to happiness is through being liberated from the constraints laid on us by others, not having to obey strict laws or the expectations of social stereotypes. Freedom is the liberty to do what I want to do with my time, my talents and my property and autonomy from anyone who might try to prevent me from doing just that. It is the staple of just about every Disney film – don't follow the expectations of others; follow your heart and learn to be yourself.

The cost of freedom

All of the above views were formulated in reaction to something. The thinkers in question lived in authoritarian times, marked by the overbearing influence of family, government or Church, so we can perhaps understand their instincts. But there are a number of fundamental problems with the version of freedom we have inherited from them. What happens when we cast off the shackles of social expectations and let our inner desires have free rein? It usually ends up that the strongest get their way and the weakest go to the wall in the inevitable competition for resources that ensues. The idea of freedom from the limitations of repressive forces of society or restraining state control led to the financial crash of 2008, as banks and mortgage lenders, freed from regulation that would have held personal ambition in check, ended up costing the world billions, the effects of which ended up at the doorsteps of the poorest, with lost jobs, income drying up and homes repossessed.

The big problem is this: freedom may offer personal independence, but what does it do to our relationships with each other? The goal of this view, which we might call a 'libertarian' idea of freedom, is independence, the ability to follow your heart wherever it takes you, confident that no one can stop you doing that (unless you are going to harm them or yourself). But that instantly sets you up against your neighbour, your work colleague or even your friend or partner (if you have one), as a potential curb on that freedom or, even worse, a menace to it. It makes me think of my neighbour as, at best, a limitation, but at worst, a threat to my freedom. I might like to play my music loudly on a summer's evening, but I can't because my neighbour might complain. Worse still, my neighbou might like to play music loudly on the same summer's evening and disturb my peace by doing so.

Every society tries to do two things: it tries to establish a framework for individual flourishing; it also tries to create some kind of social cohesion. This view of freedom does all right on the first of these – it does promise a certain degree of personal liberty and expression – but doesn't manage the second at all well. It really doesn't give us any good reasons to think of each other as anything more than an inconvenience to our own plans and projects. No wonder we struggle to get any sense of common values and our political debates seem to be more and more fractious.

In reality, this way of thinking about freedom is only about three hundred years old, and can mainly be found in the Western world. *Mulan* is a Disney film based on the Chinese legend of a warrior called Mulan Hu. It interpreted the main character as a Chinese girl who refused to follow social expectations, had to pretend to be a boy to fight in battles and found her true self in the process. The film bombed in China. Despite an impressive Asian cast and an attempt to nod to Eastern influences, the image of a young Chinese girl as heroically true to herself got no takers in China, the origin of the story in the first place. The Chinese referred to the Disney version as 'foreign Mulan', not recognizing her at all from the original version steeped in Confucian notions of modesty, communal loyalty and respect for the ways of the ancestors.

Not as free as we think?

The Christian path we have been exploring offers us a very different understanding of freedom from this.

It starts with the idea that we are not as free as we think we are. St Paul described human beings as 'under a yoke of slavery'[5] – that in our original state we are not very free at all. He had in mind the '*stoicheia*' that we saw in the last chapter – the mysterious powers at work in social institutions such as the Jewish Law or pagan worship. For us, it plays out differently but the underlying effect is the same. The idea of freedom of choice is all very well for reasonably affluent Westerners with a great deal of (apparent) consumer choice, but it rings hollow in parts of the world where billions of people's options are severely limited by poverty, lack of opportunity or disease.

Even for those who do have consumer choice, the more you think about it, the less freedom we actually have. Now that our lives are increasingly lived online, our personal preferences are out there, capable of being manipulated by anyone who can get hold of them. In 2018, Cambridge Analytica, a data-harvesting company (a euphemism if ever there was one, making personal information sound like bales of hay) was caught red-handed using personal data from billions of Facebook users to influence voting habits on Brexit and other key electoral campaigns. Did the Russians influence the US presidential election by creating all kinds of fake social media accounts to spread messages of support for Donald Trump and opposition to Hillary Clinton? Whether or not that particular charge is true, it is presumably a tip of a rather large iceberg. When you go online to buy anything, you then find yourself bombarded with advertisements for the thing you searched for in the first place. When we do buy, how much is it our choice? Or how much is it influenced by what we have been presented with in the meantime? There is a huge marketing and advertising industry out there to persuade you and me that we want things we don't need and that we will lose out if we don't get the upgraded version of what we already have.

Those are external factors. There are also the internal impulses that we wish we could be free of but aren't. All of us have them, even if they are different in each one. Addictions to drugs, alcohol or porn are obvious, yet most of our addictions are more subtle and hidden.

That wretched habit of anger that rises when we are crossed, that makes us say and do things we deeply regret once the moment of rage has passed. The jealousy that rears its head whenever we see that person who seems to have everything we want and think we deserve. The envy that, unchecked, might lead us subtly or brutally to bring our rivals down a peg or two if we could. The restlessness, that frustrating inability to be content with what we have, always wanting more, never happy. Anger, jealousy, discontent and the rest – we wish we could be free from them, but we can't and so we struggle on, inhibited by the habits that we desperately wish that we could kick for good.

Freedom from captivity

The last few chapters have looked at the way the Christian faith faces up to the evil rampant in our world and offers, as a radical alternative, God's solidarity with the suffering and forgiveness for the sinful. The result is freedom, but a different kind of freedom from the kind we are used to. At the time the New Testament was written, when people spoke about freedom everyone knew what it meant: freedom from slavery. In most households, there was the family and then there were the slaves. And most slaves wanted one thing – freedom from their bonded condition, to build their own family, own their own home and ply their own trade.

The early Christians offered freedom – not necessarily freedom from slavery (although that did come in time – read Paul's little gem of a letter to the wealthy Philemon, asking him to release his fellow Christian slave Onesimus), but freedom from a different kind of bondage. It was freedom from our old selves, freedom from shame, the shame at the part we have played in the injustice and sheer nastiness of the world, the shame of disgrace, the thoughtless word that broke a relationship, the mistake that ruined someone else's life. As we saw in the last chapter, for those bitterly repentant, the death and resurrection of Jesus gives an assurance of forgiveness, a clean slate and a new start.

It was also freedom from fear. The future, both then and now, can often feel uncertain – will it work out OK, will my friends or my children be all right, will I get sick, will I get the job I want? And even if I do, will it all end in the dark void of death facing every one of us at the end of the journey? But if Jesus has died and been raised from death, then a crack has appeared in the wall of death, in the frame that surrounds the picture, and the light has streamed in from the other side. If all that were true, this offered a freedom to thousands of people then, and countless millions since – a deep sense of freedom that came with forgiveness and hope of life here and now, and even beyond this short journey through life.

But the heart of this view of freedom is its purpose. It's all very well to be freed from the chains of what holds you back, but what are you going to do with that freedom?

Imagine two people sent by their (British) company to go to work in Florence. One is looking forward to Italian wine, holidays on the coast, lazy Sunday afternoons walking the Tuscan countryside. He speaks no Italian, but his job means he can get by without, so he doesn't bother. When he wakes at the weekend, he relishes the freedom to do what he wants, visiting art galleries, eating in Italian restaurants (orders made by sign language or just pointing to the menu) and dancing the night away in the fleshpots of Florence. The difficulty is that, when he has a problem or meets someone he'd like to get to know better, he cannot understand what is being said to him and cannot communicate except in sign language or with those who speak a bit of English. He feels that he is free to do what he wants with his time, talents and money but, in reality, he is limited by his inability to hold a decent conversation. He just can't communicate. He keeps making mistakes, is misunderstood and ends up isolated and friendless. He is free in one sense, but not free in another.

Now, imagine his colleague going through the same experience of relocation. This person signs up for language classes. Rather than going out to the wine bars and cinemas of Florence, she goes to her lessons, studies the vocabulary, absorbs tenses and accents and slowly learns to speak Italian. As time goes on, she finds herself able to speak the language, to be understood and to understand. She is gradually set free from the misunderstandings and mistakes that bedevilled her early attempts to communicate. She acquires freedom, but it is not the freedom to do what she feels like; in fact, initially, it doesn't feel like freedom at all, as she spends her evenings struggling with Italian nouns and verbs. But eventually, she acquires the liberty to converse, to build relationships and to talk freely. And, in time, when she does start to enjoy the wine bars, the restaurants and the country villages, she is able to enjoy them much more because she is able to talk to the people who live and work in them.

This is freedom to do something that is really worthwhile, freedom to experience life at its fullest, to be the person she is capable of being – someone not locked into a diminished type of freedom but liberated to live a fuller life in her adopted home.

The difficulty with libertarian views of freedom is that, on the one hand, they leave it up to us to decide what our freedom is to be used for and, on the other, when we are given the option, we tend to choose trivial things such as getting more money, becoming more famous or having more sex. This kind of freedom doesn't have any agreement on the purpose of human life or what makes us truly happy, so we are left to make it up for ourselves. And if we get what we set our hearts on, only to find it doesn't satisfy, tough. It's too late.

Onions and artichokes

Christianity does have a pretty sure idea of what makes us truly happy and claims to offer the freedom to be that kind of person. So far, we have found that much of the trouble in this world comes from our fearful tendency to turn inwards, to turn away from God, the source of everything that we value, everything that is good in our lives and the people he has placed around us. Our problem is the 'heart turned in on itself', as Luther put it.

When Jesus was asked the question, 'which is the greatest commandment?' – in other words, 'what is the most important thing to do in this life?' – his answer was not 'be yourself' or 'follow your dreams'. It was simple: love God and love your neighbour. The purpose of our being born into this world is to become the kind of person capable of loving God in thankfulness for all we have been given and to love our neighbours – the people God has placed alongside us in the next-door house or desk or classroom or office. When you meet people who have learnt this art, what strikes you is the lightness and gentle contentment they usually have. People who have learnt to love God do so because they are aware of how much they have received. They aren't desperate to be independent, because they know they are deeply dependent on God for every breath they breathe, for the sun on their backs and the rain that gives life. They also know they are dependent on all kinds of people around them – the farmers who grow their food, the bus driver who takes them to work, the person who makes their email server work. They have gained the priceless value of a grateful heart.

Likewise, people who have learnt to love their neighbours have lost that crippling self-consciousness that is always fearful of what others think of them. They feel no great need to post pictures of themselves having a great life or fret over how many likes they have on their social media stream. They take proper care of themselves, because they know that if they overstretch, they are no use to anyone, but they tend to be so good at anticipating the needs of others around them that they just don't have the time to get anxious about themselves. They are people who have learnt generosity – the art of giving rather than taking, the ability to let go of things to enable other people to thrive, safe in the knowledge that the best things in life aren't things at all.

So freedom turns out not to be the freedom to do what we want, because what we want is so often our biggest problem. The heroin addict is in a sense doing what he wants, but it's obvious to others that he is driven by some inner compulsion to indulge a habit that will ultimately destroy him. Our own petty jealousies, greed and self-obsession will do the same in less dramatic ways, but they will do it nonetheless. Freedom is not freedom from other people, the independence to go our way and to be ourselves. It is the freedom from anything that would stop us becoming the kind of person capable of love for God and our neighbour. It is freedom from pride, envy and greed, not the freedom to indulge them. It is freedom from the anxious, fearful isolation that comes when we pretend we are independent and don't need anyone else.

'freedom turns out not to be the freedom to do what we want, because what we want is so often our biggest problem'

This type of freedom works so much better than the other. Remember how we considered the way every society tries to square the circle of personal flourishing and social cohesion? And how libertarian freedom seems to do all right on the first (yet even that is debatable) but struggles with the second? This kind does both. It offers a life fulfilled – a life full of gratitude and generosity, rather than fear-filled self-absorption. We flourish best as people when we are in healthy relationships with others and notice every small thing that comes our way each day, being grateful for each one. Yet this sort of freedom also creates a far better social life. Imagine living in a community where you were wrapped up in thinking how to anticipate the needs of others and never had to think too much about your own needs because other people were anticipating what you need before you had to tell them.

At the same time, if my happiness depends on becoming skilled at loving other people, I need people to practise on. My neighbour becomes not a limitation or a threat to my freedom, but someone without whom I cannot become all that I am meant to be.

This type of freedom also means liberty from the external factors that stop us becoming this kind of person. It involves freedom from poverty, loneliness, an economic system that bombards us with messages that we are not complete unless we have this car, that dress, those trainers, that house.

This way, I am freed to be my true self, not a self I can find by looking inside or some secret inner 'me'. The idea of being 'true to myself' or 'finding myself' as a plea for authenticity and the pathway to personal fulfilment was fuelled by those eighteenth-century convictions that the true self in a state of nature is pure and unsullied; that if we were able to peel off every layer of expectation laid on us by society, the artificial constructions of identity, gender, class and occupation, we would find our true selves hidden within, like a cook preparing an artichoke, peeling away the rough leaves to find the hidden tender heart inside.

Yet what if we are, in fact, more like onions than artichokes? What if, when we peel away the expectations of others, the roles we play in society, there is nothing there? What if there is no mysterious 'self' waiting to be discovered, no essence of 'me' that is stifled by the irritating other people who expect me to play roles prescribed for me? The common assumption is that we have 'selves' waiting to be found, yet maybe this idea that we have 'selves', in the same way that we have heads or arms, hearts, livers and brains, is a relatively recent notion, one rooted in our late modern, Western view of the world.

Finding our true selves

An alternative, and much more ancient view, is that our selves are not so much discovered as created. We tend to assume that we have an elusive inner 'self', a true identity given complete at birth, that then waits to be discovered and lived out. Yet what if it works differently? Of course, we are born with particular DNA, derived from our parents and ancestors. We are each created special and unique, with potential to do good and to do harm, yet from that moment on, those inner selves get shaped and moulded by what happens to us and what we choose to do. They grow and develop, just as our bodies do.

Though we start with a unique set of genes and relationships, we shape our inner selves over our lifetimes by the choices we make, the commitments we enter into, the relationships we form, the habits we let take root, the way we react to what happens to us. A newborn baby has a 'self', but

'we shape our inner selves over our lifetimes by the choices we make'

it is like putty – over a lifetime it gets squeezed and formed by what she chooses to do and what happens to her and, eventually, often gets hardened into a fixed shape – sometimes good, sometimes not so good. At the same time, our selves are bound into the rest of the human race, the families and communities into which we were born and also moulded by decisions made even before we were born – tangibly so when it comes to drug use or illness in a mother that transfers to a child in the womb or in the more subtle, hidden ways that begin to affect us from early days. As we grow, we are shaped by what happens to us and what we choose to do: broken bones or hearts, inspiring teachers, jealous or loyal friends, where our parents decide to live, the loyalties we adopt, who we marry, what job we do and so on.

We develop our selves in relation to parents, siblings, friends, teachers, colleagues, neighbours. And our likeness to and difference from these people gives us our own sense of self. We are defined by our relationships and our commitments, not by our self-directed freedom. It is the choices we make and how we react to what happens to us that determine who we are, rather than some innate identity that is waiting to be discovered.

This points up, of course, the importance of those choices and the way we react to the events that come our way. If our selves really are created by the choices we make, then we need to choose carefully. The last chapter indicated the need for a new start, losing the old self and finding a new one, orientated not inwards on ourselves, but outwards to God and our neighbour. The next two chapters will begin to explore what this means in practice and the kinds of choices and habits that could help us live a life in tune with the universe and the God who made it.

9
Why praying is dangerous

Ask a random group of people and you will find a variety of views on the spiritual side of life. There are, of course, the thoroughgoing materialists, convinced that there is nothing out there beyond what you can see, feel, touch or taste. When you die, you die, and that's it. Then, at the other end of the spectrum, there are those firmly convinced of the reality of the spirit world, the impact of the stars and their influence on our lives and who have a persistent belief in angels and ghosts (over a third of Britons say they believe in them), and the afterlife (nearly 50 per cent believe in some kind of survival beyond death). Then there are those in the middle, often happy with the label 'spiritual but not religious' – not convinced about God, spiritual beings or life after death, but definitely aware that there is a spiritual side and there is more to life than food, money and sex.

Recent years have seen an explosion of interest in the mystical and transcendent. The term 'New Age' embraces a huge range of beliefs and practices, some involving belief in the supernatural or that humanity is about to enter a new phase of spiritual powers, often linked with scientific and psychological research, and most of it concerned with personal spiritual development. Fascination with the paranormal, extra-sensory perception, astrology and tarot readings continues to grow, to the frustration of the materialist atheists who are convinced it's all mumbo-jumbo.

Spirituality is big business. Literally. Companies like Apple, Google and Nike all offer their employees opportunities for meditation while at work, believing that it reduces stress, establishes better working relationships, enables greater enjoyment of work and therefore improves company efficiency and profits in the end. Others offer free yoga classes (the global yoga industry is said to be worth about £27bn) and numerous people today practise mindfulness to help cope with the stresses of modern life.

Back in the 1980s, when greed was good, there was perhaps less awareness of the spiritual. The rise of the new atheism was an expression of the materialist view of the world, yet even atheists these days are aware of the spiritual dimension.

Writers such as Alain de Botton and Sam Harris don't believe in God and have no truck with a supernatural world beyond the self, yet at the same time they recognize that religion does have some benefits (not least the ability to create forms of community) and stake a claim that atheists can be spiritual as well. Rather than locating the spiritual dimension 'out there' in some non-material realm beyond the self, they see it as being 'in here' – to do with an internal spiritual process of discovery. Aware of a spiritual dimension to life, the instinct is to look inside ourselves, to discover resources in inner consciousness or personal motivation to resolve questions of identity and purpose.

Yet, as we have seen already, that turn inwards is problematic. To turn inwards is inevitably to turn away from the outside, to turn our attention away from what or who stands next to us, including our neighbour, and instead to prioritize personal growth and fulfilment.

No wonder that there is, at the same time as all this enthusiasm, a rising cynicism about the whole field of 'spirituality'. For some it is simply a commodification of the spiritual to serve the purposes of a commercial world. One damning assessment of popular modern alternative therapy describes it as an 'easy, accessible and not too discomforting spirituality that promotes individual and corporate success with little cost to a modern western consumerist lifestyle'.[1] It's a way of having your materialist cake and eating it.

A spiritual world?

If time travel were possible, imagine inviting someone from the year 1850 to visit one of the major cities in the world today and trying to explain the internet to them. You might describe how there is this invisible realm all around us, available almost anywhere, that holds an unimaginable amount of information and enables us to do all kinds of things we couldn't do without it. It can tell us how to build a shed or what the capital of Peru is. It enables us to go shopping without leaving our armchair, to read all kinds of books without touching a sheet of paper and to play endless games. It makes it possible to communicate with people anywhere in the world at the touch of a button or to view live pictures from remote locations in other continents. It doesn't replace the physical world we see around us, but it really does exist alongside it.

When your confused time traveller asks for proof that it exists, you have to explain how you can't see it, feel it, touch it, smell it or taste it – in fact, your normal senses are pretty useless when it comes to accessing it. If you rely on using them, you will never discover it, however hard you try. You can see the computers, data centres, routers, servers and the miles of cables stretching across land and under the sea, not to mention the satellites in space that enable the internet to work, although they are only the infrastructure that enables it – not the real thing. But seeing them doesn't get you into the internet. To access it, you need special apparatus – a phone, a computer, a tablet. They act like a kind of portal, so that if you have one of these, this mysterious world opens up before you. You then have to learn how to navigate your way around it and make the most of its possibilities, so that you can use it wisely. You have to beware though – the internet gives you all kinds of positive opportunities that enhance ordinary life, but there is also a dark side to it, and parts you really don't want to visit because dangerous things lurk there.

Our nineteenth-century visitor would find that hard to believe. Yet in other ways they might make sense of it because it is not that dissimilar from what most people believed at the time and many still do believe today: that there is a whole realm beyond what we can immediately see and touch, far bigger than we could ever imagine, that opens up all kinds of possibilities, yet also has a light and a dark side to it.

Just like the internet, our normal senses are not much immediate use in accessing this world, although they can point to it. In the same way we can see the cables that carry data, we can explore the many institutions that claim to hold the spiritual life – churches, mosques, temples, priests and so on, but they too are the bare bones – necessary, but only the clumsy bearers of something more significant and alive.

For centuries, the human race longed to overcome the limitations of geography – that is what lay behind the great periods of exploration that took travellers from their homelands to discover distant horizons. Yet was there a way to see different places and communicate with far-flung peoples more quickly, especially for people who didn't have the luxury of being able to leave their homes, families and jobs for long periods? Sooner or later, the human race would surely find a way to do it. Similarly, countless people, looking up at the stars on a cloudless night or feeling the emptiness of having everything they needed but knowing it was not enough, have noticed that all the material goods in the world don't always satisfy a deeper, 'spiritual' need for something more. They too have longed for the ability to communicate not just with other people across the world, but with whatever, whoever, might be out there beyond everything that we see.

The great religions of the world have always suggested there is another dimension beyond the material. They have also said that you need particular apparatus to access it. In the Christian approach to this, what you need are not sight, taste or touch, nor even laptops or phones, but things like prayer, the Bible, worship alongside other people, bread and wine, and the waters of baptism – these are the portals to the world of the Spirit. They are the means by which the new self is built and reshaped. And if anyone is to begin to take the first tentative steps down this pathway, sooner or later they will need to start to pray.

Of course, if you don't believe in God, you might think at this point that what I'm referring to here is just for religious people. Yet prayer is a deep human instinct. Even atheists pray when they are desperate. Might it just be that a whispered prayer could be the start of a relationship with a God you don't yet believe in? Most atheists or agnostics who become Christians started with a hesitant, hopeful prayer to someone out there who might or might not be listening. The heart of Christianity is not an abstract conviction that there is a divine being who made the world, but is beginning an ongoing relationship with that God – and it always starts with talking to him, however falteringly or feebly.

The spirituality of the blender

If you are going to learn how to pray, you need to start by admitting you don't know how to do it. We all pray when we are desperate, but prayer when everything is going fine doesn't come naturally to us. As with most valuable things in life, such as learning to play the violin or mending watches, a basic desire to learn has to submit to discipline and being taught by those who have become masters of it.

Part of the problem with much of what goes under the name of 'spirituality' in modern life is that it tries to choose various bits that it happens to like from a number of spiritual traditions of the past, while leaving aside the less attractive parts. Personal spirituality often resembles a fruit smoothie mixed in a blender – a statue of the

Buddha, a little Native American wisdom, a touch of feng shui, a whiff of incense, all mixed together to make you feel peaceful and more in tune with the world. The goal of all this is usually some sense of personal serenity or calmness, yet this is typically far from what the spiritual traditions of the past had in mind.

Many people adopt quasi-Buddhist practices, as these promise stillness and a step towards feeling better about yourself. The irony is that, ultimately, Buddhism believes that the self is an illusion and aims at its annihilation, not its realization. In the Buddha's 'Setting in Motion the Wheel of Dharma', taught to his followers soon after his enlightenment, he offered a 'middle path' between self-indulgence – sex, drugs and rock 'n' roll – and self-mortification, neither of which, he says, lead to happiness. He introduced the 'Four Noble Truths'. The first is the inescapable *fact* of suffering and affliction. Bad stuff happens, there's nothing you can do about it, and there is no hope or expectation that it will ever be otherwise. The second is the *cause* of suffering: desire or attachment to things within this world. The third pinpoints the *means* of dealing with such desire: learning to contain and ultimately extinguish desire. And the fourth describes the *goal* of this path: the end of desire and the resultant release from suffering. Ultimately, the goal is the extinction not only of desire, but even of the individual who desires. At the moment of his enlightenment under the Bodhi tree, it is significant that the Buddha did not say, 'I am liberated', but, 'It is liberated' – he had gone beyond himself and his own separate identity had been extinguished.

Now this is not to say this is right or wrong. It is to say that you can't have it both ways. Many secular-minded people in the West today are motivated by the longing for rich, exotic experience and are on the spiritual search to discover themselves. They have no great interest in the idea of the extinction of desire or the self, however much they may be attracted by the more superficial attractions of a bit of

Buddhist-lite meditation. The desire for self-realization doesn't sit very well with the Buddhist goal of self-extinction.

Christianity does not aim at the elimination of desire – in fact, it says that desire for God and desire for those we love is at the heart of the mystery of existence. We never get beyond desire and love, because they are what life is all about. There is a kind of transcendence of the self in Christianity, but it is a reorientating rather than extinguishing of the self towards love for the neighbour, by enabling us to begin to feel the glimmers of delighting in them, however unlikely that may seem to start with. Christianity is all about the possibility of changing our desires, not eliminating them. Jesus doesn't teach us to extinguish ourselves or even to be ourselves, but to realize our true selves by giving ourselves in love for God and our neighbours.

This jumbled approach is perhaps typical of an age that always thinks it knows better than the past, but is a bit like thinking that it would be a good idea to learn another language and deciding to mix German verbs, Spanish tenses, French grammar, Portuguese nouns and Arabic verbs. You might prefer Portuguese nouns to Latin ones, but the result will be highly idiosyncratic and not make a great deal of sense. That's not the way languages work and, as Ludwig Wittgenstein, among others, pointed out, religions operate like a language in having a set of practices that make sense in relation to one another and to the underlying beliefs that hold the thing together. Similarly, each spiritual path is based on a particular set of beliefs about human nature, about God and about the world, and therefore that path has an integrity within itself which doesn't quite work if you try to blend several together.

To think we know better than the ancients who over centuries developed the spiritual traditions of prayer found in the different methods of religious practice is, not to put too fine a point on it, a trifle arrogant. Whatever we come up with might bring us a sense of momentary peace, but it is unlikely to have the long-term effect that the deeper traditions of spirituality were meant to. Prayer was never meant to be a technique to de-stress, to find personal tranquillity (although that might be a by-product), but aimed at nothing less than a growing, intimate connection with God our Maker, the Love that brought the world into being and, as a result, the transformation of character from within – the growth of our new selves into maturity.

Mindful prayer

One of the most popular forms of contemporary spirituality is mindfulness. Mindfulness is everywhere. If you are stressed, it is likely that, sooner or later, your friends, your employer, your school or even a local doctor will recommend you engage in some kind of mindful activity. And it's not just a fad – there is an increasing body of scientific research showing the psychological benefits of mindful practice in reducing stress, and promoting better health, quality of relationships and greater productivity.

Prayer has many things in common with mindfulness; in a way it could be called a form of mindful activity (or perhaps better, mindfulness is a form of prayer). Prayer, like mindfulness, is at least in part a moment when you step back from the normal activity of life, conscious of yourself and God, as you interact with your surroundings and become aware of what is happening around you, both what you can see and what you can't. It is a chance to recognize that you are not your desires or emotions. That what you instinctively feel you want or need may not be what you actually want or need, and that it is a mistake to necessarily identify your inner identity with your feelings or longings.

If mindfulness has been described as 'paying attention in a particular way: on purpose, in the present moment, and non-judgmentally',[2] that has a lot in common with Christian prayer. In fact, mindfulness has been described not as being specific to any particular religious tradition, but instead, 'far from being the exclusive possession of any particular religion or ideology, (it) is a universal quality of attention, available to all human beings'.[3] If that is the case, the question is not whether we exercise mindfulness, but what kind do we exercise? What are the assumptions we bring to the practice of mindful attitudes to life? What are we trying to be mindful of?

Prayer involves becoming conscious of God and the world around you. In the stories told in the Gospels, Jesus often stops to notice particular things that might otherwise be missed – seeds germinating secretly and silently in the soil, a sparrow falling to the ground, a widow putting a tiny coin into the collection box. At one point, Jesus tells his followers to stop and pay attention to the birds and to the flowers growing at the edges of the fields, and the way in which, despite the fact that they don't work hard for their living, God provides for them.[4] He goes on to say (in one modern translation): 'Give your entire attention to what God is doing right now, and don't get worked up about what may or may not happen tomorrow. God will help you deal with whatever hard things come up when the time comes.'[5]

These examples show a particular kind of mindfulness. Jesus doesn't just notice things; he notices them in relation to the God of love who made them. The seed germinating in the ground is not just a miracle in itself, it is a picture of how the kingdom of God grows in the world, often unnoticed and yet making a large impact in the end. The sparrow that dies is one among thousands, yet Jesus points out how every single one is known and recognized by the God who made them. It becomes a pointer to God's affection for each individual part of the creation. A widow's small gift is significant not just in what she gives but in the level of sacrifice it involves. In pure economic terms, it is a paltry gift yet, in fact, it is more significant in the eyes of God than any other, because it represents almost all she owns – it is a picture of self-sacrificial generosity such as that we find in the heart of God.

This is a relational, rather than just a technical form of mindfulness. It starts not with our decision to try to be a bit more mindful, but with the idea that before we ever decide to do anything, we are held in existence by a hand of love. One of the Psalms says: 'what are human beings that you are mindful of them, mortals that you care for them?'[6] This kind of attentiveness begins not with our mindful activity but with the extraordinary insight that before you ever thought of being mindful, God is mindful of you – that he thinks of you and holds you in his heart at every moment, even now while you are reading these words.

It is similar with the practice of gratitude. Mindfulness instruction often stresses the need for gratitude and offers exercises to generate thankfulness for the simple things in life. Many psychological studies suggest the beneficial effects of a grateful approach to life. People dogged by resentment and grievance about how badly life has treated them have discovered the ability to express appreciation of others or to let minor insults pass as a result of the practice of being grateful for the ordinary things – a roof over their heads, clean air to breathe, trees in the park or a kind word from a friend.

Yet there is something a little odd about being grateful to nothing in particular or, at most, to an inanimate object, such as a tree for existing or a river for flowing past, as neither has chosen to do so. Pressing this further, Bob Emmons, Professor of Psychology at UC Davis in California, who has done extensive studies on gratitude, points out the distinction between gratitude and thankfulness. We tend to be grateful *for something*, but thankful *to someone*. Gratitude is the ability to recognize good things in our lives that are not self-generated or even deserved, because if they were, there would be no point in being grateful for them – we would be thanking ourselves, which doesn't make much sense. Gratitude is therefore one of those emotions that turns us outwards from our self-absorption and the idea that we are somehow self-sufficient in our independence, to recognize that we are thoroughly dependent on others beyond ourselves for all that makes our lives enjoyable and fruitful. Gratitude is the ability to see something good in our lives as a thing we didn't make or deserve, but that instead is a gift we have received.

But a gift implies a giver. For a gift to be a gift, in other words, an act of generosity and love, it needs to be deliberately given by someone. A box of chocolates given directly to me by a friend means much more than just finding a random box left in the street outside my house. Gifts that come from a giver, deliberately chosen and given personally, mean more than things that would be there whether or not we existed.

Gratitude therefore needs to grow into thankfulness. While a sense of gratitude can be psychologically beneficial, it is richer when it is expressed as thankfulness to something or someone who has given the gift to us. Christian prayer (or mindfulness, if you prefer) tells me that the tree outside my window is not just there, but is a gift from a heavenly Father who made it and gave it, not just randomly, but in some sense, at least in this moment, to me as the person observing it right now. As author G. K. Chesterton put it, 'If my children wake up on Christmas morning and have someone to thank for putting candy in their stockings, have I no one to thank for putting two feet in mine?'[7] If there is no Giver, then gratitude is still better than resentment, but we are doing all the work, the transaction is just from our side. If, behind the gift, there is someone who thought of us and decided to give it, the gift becomes something richer – a sign of a greater love, a deeper reality behind the gift itself. A gift we receive is never really about the gift – it's about the relationship established between us and the one who gave it. As we say, it's the thought that counts or, perhaps even better, it's the person who counts.

These examples of the way in which the significance of ordinary things is enriched when seen in relation to God, and the way in which gratitude is enhanced by being seen as thankfulness to a Giver, show how Christian prayer can be a much richer and more fruitful form of mindfulness. The habit of prayer, day after day, giving some time to pause and reflect on life in the presence of God, builds the new identity we have been discovering. It helps us realize we are people held in existence by a God who loves us; we begin to find a deep thankfulness for life and all good things taking root in our souls.

Yet there is more to prayer than this.

What's the point of asking?

Why do we pray? One answer might be to experience the presence of God.

Prayer in its various forms is the primary way into the world of the spirit, that extra dimension of life all around us, yet not immediately accessible to our normal senses. Christians say that the desire to pray arises not primarily because of some internal spiritual need to do so, but because God himself is constantly nudging us to come to him. This is the reality of the Holy Spirit, who is God present and engaging with us now. When Jesus left his disciples, he promised a gift – that while he would no longer be physically present to them, he would send them a 'helper' or a 'counsellor' – the Holy Spirit who would continue to enable them to experience his presence until his promised return. If and when you feel the urge to pray, that is the Holy Spirit nudging and urging you to do so.

Prayer is sometimes powerfully transformative. Many Christians experience goose bumps at the presence of the Holy Spirit when someone lays hands on them and prays for them. For others, it happens mainly through coming to Holy Communion and receiving the bread and wine. At other times, it might be through solitary contemplative meditation over a sustained period of time or, again, it might be through hearing a particularly insightful sermon or reading a section of the Bible that seems to speak in a powerfully personal and direct way.

Yet there are times when you pray and you feel nothing. Powerful spiritual experiences help, because they are a reassurance that there is something there, yet they are not the main point. Something deeper is going on.

Christians have always believed that prayer is more than a psychological technique to enhance our experience of life – it actually changes the world. Talk to any Christians and they will recount stories or prayers that have been answered in ways that seem far more than coincidence. Just as God brings about his will for the world through human acts of compassion, scientific research that produces medicine, the work of lawyers that bring justice or of doctors that bring health, so God somehow weaves our prayers into the way the world works and grows.

There is something essentially mysterious about this. Anyone looking for a neat formula that a certain amount of prayer will produce a corresponding amount of response, will be disappointed. Lots of the time, you pray (for someone's healing, for example) and nothing happens. But just occasionally, something remarkable does: prayers for healing receive a sudden unexpected answer or desperately needed funds appear in the nick of time. What do we make of this?

I don't have an answer.[8] And I think it's important that I don't have an answer, because prayer is essentially personal, not contractual. We don't know why God answers some prayers with a yes and others with a no, just as a young child does not always understand why a parent seems to respond to some requests and not others. While God does occasionally seem to answer prayers in the way we would like him to, that is not the ultimate point of it. If it was, the inevitable question would arise as to why we need to do it at all, given that presumably God knows what we need before we ask him.

Yet there is perhaps something we can say.

There is a scene towards the end of Nikos Kazantzakis' novel, *The Last Temptation of Christ*, where the sick of Judea pelt Jesus with their bandages and crutches as he carries the cross towards Golgotha, because he has failed to heal them all in answer to their prayers. So why doesn't God answer each one of our prayers for healing or divine intervention?

At the risk of simplification, Christians believe three things about God:

1 that he made the world with a certain order, a structure of cause and effect, with a moral regularity to it, where actions carry consequences and responsibilities;
2 that this world has now been damaged, allowing the virus of evil to enter it, seeking to destroy all that he has created;
3 that God still loves the world and is at work to rescue it, by sending his Son to live, die and rise again within that world, and promising that he will one day restore it.

Given all this, what would we expect in terms of God's interaction with the world?

In one of Douglas Coupland's novels, one of the characters, Lloyd Anway, ponders a Christian group that expects frequent miracles:

> they talk about miracles all the time, and this, too, baffles me. They're always asking for miracles, and finding them everywhere. In as much as I am a spiritual man, I do believe in God – I think that he created an order for the world; I believe that, in constantly bombarding him with requests for miracles, we are also asking that he unravel the fabric of the world. A world of continuous miracles would be a cartoon, not a world.[9]

He has a point. A world of continuous miracles, every casual prayer answered, would be a very unpredictable and unreliable one, a place where you could never tell the results of certain actions and in which any kind of moral structure or regularity was absent. A world in which God intervened every time something bad was about to happen would be a world in which we never learnt the habits and virtues that lead to good and healthy human life, because you could never predict what the results of any particular action would be.

But a world without any miracles at all would be a world that God had apparently abandoned to its own devices. It would be a world that God winds up like a watch and allows to run its own course while he turns his attention elsewhere. This would naturally lead to the conclusion that the God who made this world could not really care much about it.

Maybe this pattern, of specific and visible answers to prayer (for example, for healing that cannot be explained by normal medical processes), which are by definition rare, occasional but real, is precisely what we should expect given the Christian understanding of God and creation – a God who creates a world with regular physical and moral order, a world that has become damaged, and yet a world that God still loves and promises to redeem.

In John's Gospel, miracles are described as *semeia* – signs. In other words, their significance is not found in themselves, but in what they point to. When a person is healed through prayer, it is, of course, good for that person and perhaps an encouragement to the person who offers the prayer, but the significance of the miracle is something much greater. It is a sign, pointing both to the power of God that lies behind this remarkable occurrence, and to that day when all sickness will be banished.

Turning towards the light

Do we pray in order to experience God? Or to change things? Well, we do both. But ultimately prayer is about something more. George MacDonald, a Scottish writer who had a great influence on C. S.

Lewis's journey towards Christianity, once wrote this about prayer:

> If God is so good as you represent him, and if he knows all that
> we need and better far than we do ourselves, why should it be
> necessary to ask him for anything? I answer, What if he knows
> prayer to be the thing we need first and most? What if the main
> object in God's idea of prayer be the supplying of our great, our
> endless need – the need of Himself? . . . Hunger may drive the
> runaway child home, and he may or may not be fed at once, but
> he needs his mother more than his dinner. Communion with
> God is the one need of the soul beyond all other need: prayer is
> the beginning of that communion.[10]

Prayer is one of the most vital ways of being orientated away from
ourselves and towards God. And when we do that, whether we feel it
or not, something happens.

During the night, when darkness reigns, flowers tend to curl up,
go into themselves, shrink back, perhaps to cope with the colder
temperatures, perhaps to prevent pollen from becoming heavy with
dew. When the sun rises and warms the air, the flower begins to open
again, to reveal its true colours, leaning towards the sun. It's a picture of the way the Holy Spirit works on people. As we consciously
orientate ourselves towards God in prayer, worship, study, fasting or
any of the other disciplines of the spiritual life, we find the Holy Spirit opening us up, reversing that 'turned-in' nature, warming us and
shaping our new selves.

If you start seriously to pray, you risk opening yourself to the light.
You risk allowing that light to shine into the darker places of your
soul. You risk the sometimes-painful process of being opened out
and changing in a profound way, changing into your new, your true
self that can only emerge in relation to God.

When you pray, you tend to notice people's pain a bit more, the
anguish that lies behind other people's perhaps hostile behaviour.

Dwelling on the sufferings of the world or even of your sick elderly neighbour can get you down, but dwelling on them in the presence of God gives hope that suffering is temporary, yet also makes you understand that pain a little better because you have tried to imagine what it is like. True prayer will draw you deeper into the places of pain in the world. It might make you leave your job. It might cause you to volunteer to visit a prison, a homeless centre or a foodbank.

Prayer will make your heart soft. Hard hearts are sometime easier to live with, as they don't get broken, whereas soft ones do. Prayer is dangerous. But worth it.

There will be people reading this who may be thinking: 'That's all very well, and I can see it makes some kind of sense, but, then again, it doesn't provide me with proof, so how do I decide? Even if part of me would like to believe, I can't make myself believe something I don't, so what do I do? How can I pray if I'm not sure God even exists?'

In one of his *Pensées*, the French writer Blaise Pascal imagines a person in exactly this dilemma, trying to decide whether to gamble on believing in God or remaining in unbelief: 'My hands are tied . . . I am forced to wager but I am so made that I cannot believe. What do you want me to do then?' Pascal then goes on to describe those who have come to believe and outlines how they started: 'They behaved just as if they did believe.'[11]

His advice is this: if you can't quite convince yourself, but suspect there may be some truth in it and would quite like to believe, then start living as if you did. In other words, start praying to God as if he is really there, even if you're not sure he is. Start reading the Bible as if it really is God speaking directly to you, listening for what he might say. Treat each person you meet today as if they are someone created by God and therefore precious and of ultimate value, even if you don't like them. Start living as Jesus has overcome death and therefore anything that threatens life. And start meeting with other Christians as if that community really is the place where you will grow in all this and learn to play your part in God's plan to change the world.

There is a famous scene in the film *Indiana Jones and the Last Crusade*, where Harrison Ford is seeking the Holy Grail. His path passes through a tunnel into an opening in the side of a cliff over a yawning chasm. The guidebook he is using tells him that the only way forward is to step out into the apparently empty space above the chasm. As he does, as he trusts himself to the void, a bridge suddenly opens up under his feet, leading him to safety on the other side. That is a picture of faith and how it works. Faith is never certainty, but the more you exercise it, the more you feel firm ground under your feet. Just try it.

10
Why we can't live alone

We have never been more connected. Yet we have never felt more alone. The extraordinary revolution in communication that has taken place over the past fifty years has enabled us to be in touch with each other instantly across continents in ways that our grandparents could never have imagined. During the lockdown of the COVID-19 pandemic we depended on virtual communication like never before. Social media has given everyone a voice and access to all kinds of other voices. Facebook's corporate mission is 'to give people the power to build community and bring the world closer together'. Twitter offers ordinary people the opportunity to 'start a global conversation'. You would have thought the result would be a more united, transparent, kinder world.

Yet all the evidence suggests that loneliness is rampant in our societies. A recent survey said that almost half of all Americans felt at times excluded, isolated or lonely. Nine million people in the UK say that they 'often or always' feel lonely and more than half of adults feared that no one would notice for a long time if they suddenly disappeared. Half a million older people go at least five or six

'more than half of adults feared that no one would notice for a long time if they suddenly disappeared'

days a week without seeing or speaking to anyone at all, with half of people over 75 living alone, many going for weeks without seeing anyone else. Experts on loneliness describe it as more a state of mind than a comment on your social life. It is possible to be surrounded by people, especially if you live in a large city, or even to have many friends, yet be lonely. If you *feel* lonely and think that no one really understands you or watches out for you, then you *are* lonely.

It is tempting to blame social media, because it replaces 'real' relationships with virtual ones, yet all it has done is to allow what is inside our heads and hearts to become more visible. Twitter effectively enables us to read each other's minds. Before social media, we all had thoughts and ideas, but most of us either let them remain there or spoke about them to a few friends. Now we have the opportunity to let the world hear those thoughts and opinions. It's not that the thoughts have got worse, it's just that we can now see much more readily the mixture of genuine kindness and murky spite that resides inside all of our hearts. The result is a more fractious and polarized public space, and a race to parade perfect lives before others that only leads to an increasing sense of inadequacy and the resulting feeling of isolation.

Faced with this loneliness, we long for community. Yet that word is one of the most overworked in our vocabulary. A bit like 'love', it is similar to a worn coin – so overused that you can hardly make out what it looks like any more. The overuse points to something though – our desperate longing for it. The notion of freedom we looked at in an earlier chapter offers the dream of independence, following my own personalized pathway in life, following my dreams wherever they take me. However, along with that comes an inevitable sense of isolation. We may be intent on independence, but that tends not to be very compatible with building strong bonds of community. We can't have it both ways.

We need togetherness, but not just to make us feel better. We need community if we are going to live differently. Kurt Vonnegut, the American novelist and artist, once wrote: 'What should young people do with their lives today? Many things, obviously. But the most daring thing is to create stable communities in which the terrible disease of loneliness can be cured . . .'[1] We need community as the base from which to fight the evils that diminish life and destroy relationships. The start of an answer to the evil in the world is to form communities that can tackle it head on.

We have spent a fair bit of time looking at evil, suffering and death in this book, because it is not only the big question that Christianity faces, but the big question all of us face in navigating our way through life. Death may have been defeated on Easter Day, but it refuses to go quietly. It still stalks us and, despite the promise of life beyond it still lurks in the shadows and sends reminders that it is still there, in every sickness, national conflict or careless act that destroys a friendship.

Ultimately, while we can debate the reasons for evil, the key question is how we deal with it when it comes our way, as it surely will. How will we find the resources to endure it or even confront it when we see it? What is sure is that we cannot do it alone.

Peaceful resistance

In June 1940, the Nazis invaded France and took control. They spread the message that they were now in charge and that resistance was futile. Swastikas hung from the Eiffel Tower and German troops patrolled the streets of Paris. It seemed there was nothing that the French could do about the hostile power that had taken over. Yet there were some who refused to give in. They formed small cells of people who never recognized Nazi rule, kept loyal to the ideal of a liberated France and did all they could to resist the evil regime. They sang French songs, circulated books and magazines that kept alive a vision of a free country, attacked enemy interests wherever they could, lived extraordinarily disciplined lives to keep focused and avoid capture, and waited expectantly for the day when someone would come and liberate their land.

The Resistance is an image of what the Church is meant to be. We live in a world still stalked by the remnants of an alien power – the power of evil that lurks in each of our hearts and plays itself out in the destruction of the planet, the abuse of the vulnerable and the ordinary petty ways in which we hurt each other day after day. We see that power at work in those iron laws we mentioned in an earlier chapter – that only the thin, the pretty and the wealthy count, that your value is directly related to your popularity or measure of fame, that we are locked in a competitive race for money, influence and power that determines whether we are winners or losers, that happiness comes from consuming stuff, which depends on having enough cash to get what you want.

The good news that Jesus brings is that you don't have to live like that. There is another path, another set of rules that are much more liberating and creative. There is a new world coming that we see hints of here and now, but that isn't here completely yet. The winds of winter still blow, but the promise is that spring and summer are coming. But to live like this and to keep believing it is hard to do on your own. That is why we need the Church.

You might think church is a place you go to on a Sunday, sing a few hymns, sit to listen to some readings, hear someone talk for a few minutes and then go home again. In reality, the Church was always meant to be the heart of resistance to the power of evil in the world, a community that teaches a different way to live, a place where we learn resistance to ways of life that destroy hope. The Church might not seem the front line of the battle between good and evil, but that's precisely what it's meant to be.

'the Church was always meant to be the heart of resistance to the power of evil in the world'

Of course, the Church is a mixed bag. Sometimes it gets so anxious about its own survival that it forgets what it is for. It is a perfect place to hide devious desires behind a veneer of respectability and sanctity. It shares in most, if not all, of the sins of the rest of the human race. Yet, like an oyster, what on the outside can look ugly and wrinkled, on the inside hides a precious pearl that you don't want to miss. Looking at it through the lens of being a resistance movement might help us make sense of some of the things the Church does as it enlists us as part of the resistance to the effects of evil and suffering in our world.

Everything has a message

All around us every day there are institutions that train us subtly to think and to act in a certain way. Think for a moment of the way a shopping mall works. As you go in, you notice big glass windows, displaying an enticing array of things to buy. Food outlets appeal to your sense of smell, bright colours stimulate your vision, feel-good music plays in the stores that soothes or excites in equal measure. You venture into a clothes store that displays pictures of good-looking, mainly younger people, smiling or laughing on a beach, maybe, surrounded by similarly happy faces, offering a picture of what the good life is, wearing (of course) the brand of the shop you're in.

When you look at these pictures, you are meant to feel a combination of inadequacy and desire – the realization that your life doesn't match the person on the beach, but you would like it to. Don't you want to be one of those happy people? Buy our stuff and you will. Shopping encourages comparison. Will I look better in this jacket or that one? The mall tells you all the time that what you have is not good enough. You may have all the clothes you need in your wardrobe at home, but it's last year's fashion or doesn't quite fit or you just see something you like better. It values obsolescence – the idea that the things you have, even though they would last perfectly well for years to come if you had no option but to wear them, are old hat and you need something more, despite the environmental problems created by the constant production of goods and the plastic packaging that comes with them.

Shopping malls are not evil. There's no harm in visiting them and buying things there. The point is to listen carefully to the sermons that they preach. They are not neutral. They have a message. It is rarely explicit but is always there, and it runs like this: *you are not OK as you are and shopping will make it (and you) better.* The gaping hole in your life can be filled with things you can buy here in this store. Salvation and healing are found through spending. It's why we talk, half-jokingly, of retail *therapy.* Shopping malls, focused around the retail experience, encourage comparisons with others, persuade us that our value is found in how we look and foster an endless search for novelty.[2]

You could do a similar exercise for any cultural institution, such as modern universities (designed to produce competitive, successful consumers who will get well-paid jobs and become leaders in society) or certain businesses (which see increasing share value as the fundamental measure of success and often value the person who gives their all to the company rather than the one who puts their family and other relationships first). All the communities in which we spend our time have a set of spoken or unspoken values. None is neutral. They are all religious, in the sense that they each have an idea of what matters most, what you should set your heart on and a set of practices that enables you to keep your focus on that goal and achieve it.

So it turns out that the Church is not the only religious community in town. Like the shopping mall, the university and every business, it has a goal of the kind of person it is trying to produce. It is trying to teach us how to love God and, out of that, to learn to love ourselves properly, to love our neighbours and even our enemies. The rest of this chapter tries to explain how church, rather than being a boring way to spend a Sunday morning, is, in fact, the front line of resistance to all that destroys life and love. It is a worldwide movement, expressed in small local communities to help us play our part in God's resistance to all that destroys life.

Loving God

According to Christianity, the purpose of life is to learn to love God and your neighbour. It is to become someone full of gratitude and generosity, receiving and giving in a natural rhythm of healthy living and ultimately dying, which is the gateway to an even fuller and richer life beyond death. If you only ever receive, you become self-orientated and bloated. If you only ever give, you become empty and exhausted. We need to do both.

There is a natural link between these two. Blaise Pascal wrote this:

> There was once in humanity a true happiness, yet all that now remains of it is an empty void and trace. We try in vain to fill it with everything around us ... The problem is that none of them can help, since this void can only be filled by something infinite and unchangeable: in other words, by God himself.[3]

That void, the dissatisfaction, the unease, the sense of dislocation that many of us feel in our most honest moments, was only ever meant to be filled by the God who gave us life in the first place, because we are wired to flourish only when we are loved. The starting point in learning to love God and neighbour is allowing the love that lies at the heart of God, the love that gave birth to the universe, the love that we see fleshed out in Jesus Christ, to begin to dwell deep in your soul.

So often our inability to love others is rooted in our fear that we will lose out. If we make ourselves vulnerable, we will get hurt. If we give away money or possessions, we will lose them for ever. If we give our time to the unlovely, we will miss out on the people who really matter. There are so many voices around us saying that we are too fat, too ugly, too ordinary, too boring, to be of any value. We learnt to internalize those voices from an early age and the result is a yearning, desperate attempt to prove ourselves worth the attention of others. It's why we spend so much time measuring our sense of worth by the number of followers or likes we get on social media.

If you are convinced in your heart that the one thing that matters about you above all else is that you are loved with an everlasting love – that there is nothing that you can suffer that puts you beyond the love of God, and that there is nothing you can do, however bad, that puts you beyond the reach of the forgiveness of God – the more that becomes the bedrock of your self-image and identity, the more you will find the security to love other people around you. If not even dying can separate you from that love, then it becomes a force at work in your heart and mind that can help you overcome all the smaller obstacles on the road of life.

But how does this love put down roots in our souls? How does its releasing power work its way into the dark hidden recesses of our lives, opening up the parts that are hurting and closed? How do we get changed from being part of the problem of the world to part of the solution? Church, with all its flaws and frustrations, its moments of awe and mystery, is the place we go to be taken back, week after regular week, to that love that will not let us go, to open ourselves, together with others, to the Holy Spirit who opens us out as the sun does to a daytime flower.

That love comes to us in words. Each time we meet, part of the Bible – a library of books that tells the story of that love – is read out and someone has the job of offering some explanation, a deeper reading of that part of the story. It comes to us in something you can actually feel and taste: when we gather (in some churches it's every week, in others less often, but still considered important) we share bread and wine, which offers the gift of God's love embodied in this sign of the very flesh and blood of Jesus Christ. It comes to us as we express grati-tude: whenever we meet, we always take time to offer prayers of thanks-giving, reminding ourselves of the things we have received over the past week – family, food, work, neighbours, sunshine, rain and the rest. It comes to us in music as we sing songs of worship and praise to God.

Sometimes people wonder why, if God is so great, he needs us to worship him? After all, if I insisted that my friends and family kept telling me how wonderful I am, that would not be a sign of wisdom but of insecurity. Yet the reason we sing songs and utter words of praise to God is not that he needs it but that *we* need it – and God knows that we need it, which is why he asks us to do it. We need to be constantly reminded of the goodness and faithfulness of God, espe-cially when there are so many voices around telling us that he either doesn't exist or that, if he does, he is dull or, even worse, monstrous. Songs, with music that can speak to the heart in a way that few other things can, are a way to do exactly that.

As we hear, see, taste and sing of the love of God, the Holy Spirit opens us out to God. If evil is the absence of good, then learning to love Goodness and the God who is the source of all goodness is the first step to resisting the evil of the world.

Loving yourself

We have seen some of the ways in which our culture breeds narcis-sism, an unhealthy self-obsession that turns our attention away from God and each other. There is, however, a proper kind of self-love, one that involves a healthy sense of self-knowledge and awareness of the impact that we have on the world.

If we are tempted to think we are primarily consumers, justified by our role in keeping the economy growing, we need constant re-minders of who we really are: children loved by a Father who made us and has a purpose for us. In many churches, there is a habit of what is called 'sharing the peace', a part of the service where people go around (when social distancing rules allow) shaking hands or giving brief hugs as a way of saying that everyone matters, everyone is important to God and this community. It is an expression of the value of each person, young or old, as part of the whole. Many churches also offer the opportunity for someone to pray with those who come to the gathering burdened by something – an illness, a family member in trouble or a difficulty at work.

It doesn't matter how rich or poor you are, what your ethnicity, gender or abilities – when you come forward for Holy Communion, you get given the same bread and wine as everyone else. There is no fast track, no gold standard service for those who put a bit more in the collection plate. The bread and wine are not just wafted generally in the direction of the people, but offered to each individual, usually placed into your hands if you want it, as a sign that you are a beloved, precious creation, yet also in need of help, forgiveness and grace. That simple action, holding up empty hands and receiving the gift of bread and wine, tells me whenever I take it that I am valued, special, worthy – not because of my talents or achievements, but simply because my Creator loves me.

At the same time, self-love is not self-indulgence. It also involves a dose of realism, recognizing our complicity in the evils of the world. Resistance fighters dared not let their guard drop for a moment in case they betrayed a friend, let plans slip to the enemy or were identified as a member of the opposition to Nazi rule. They also had to stay focused on their primary role of fighting the German army and not be distracted from it.

Before it tackles the iniquities of the world outside the Church, resistance needs to start with the evil inside our own hearts or even within the Church. Sometimes people ask why, if God is opposed to evil, he does not eliminate it from the world overnight. Presumably he could destroy all the causes of evil within his world, so why doesn't he go ahead and do it? The problem is that if he were to do so, none of us would survive the cull. We are part of the problem. Jesus tells a story of a farmer who sowed seed in a field, only for a rival to secretly sow weeds in the same field to destroy the crop. His workers come and ask him if they should pull up the weeds, but the farmer says no – the weeds have become so entangled with the stalks of wheat that if they pull them up, they will destroy both. He tells them to wait until the harvest, when the final work of disentangling the good wheat from the useless weeds can happen. It's a story that makes a simple point: good and evil are often entangled in this world and in our own hearts, it's not always easy to tell them apart and it takes time for them to be separated.

This is why the Christian life is a life of discipline and a certain degree of self-examination. Thus, when we come together, we often take a moment to confess our sins – to look inside in a brief time of self-scrutiny, to bring to the surface anything we have done that has colluded with the enemy powers. It is also meant to be a chance for the church community to examine itself too, to see if there are flaws that need addressing, broken relationships that need healing. That moment of confession is a rare one in modern life – a moment where we are invited to reflect on where we might have hurt or damaged others, to lament our part in the destruction of this planet, to do the work of identifying and resisting the habits of harm that have taken root in us.

The Church is also meant to be a place where the depths of evil and suffering can be spoken of safely, where they can be looked squarely in the eye, because we know that they are not the last word. A little while ago, an elderly relative got in touch with me, asking me to take her funeral and giving me all kinds of instructions as to what should happen at her death. She was in good health and sound of mind, and her church had run a course for elderly people, helping them prepare for death. It seemed to me a right and proper Christian thing to do – speaking of death calmly, even nonchalantly, because we know it's not the worst thing that can happen and is, in fact, the gateway to even greater life beyond. Church does not always have to be a place of joy and laughter. It should also be a place of tears, of real sorrow at the pain and distress caused by sickness or bereavement; a place where people can cry together and mourn properly, because we know that sin and death are real enemies, though now defeated.

Loving your neighbour

Loving your neighbour is a great idea. Until you meet them. Michael Ignatieff, the Canadian philosopher, writes: 'There is no such thing as Love of the human race, only the love of this person or that, in this time and not in any other.'[4] He's right. The problem is that with lives increasingly being lived

'Loving your neighbour is a great idea. Until you meet them.'

online, we rarely meet our actual neighbours. Online relationships, like friendships, are selective. They are based on common interests and you can always block someone you don't like. The thing about church is that it is relentlessly local and physical. Your neighbours, or at least a cross-section of them, are there every week. Thin ones, fat ones, old ones, young ones, rich ones, poor ones, black ones, white ones; people you like and people you don't.

Church can feel a bit ordinary. It is not usually full of the powerful and influential, the people who will help you get on in life. If you want to meet them, go somewhere else. Church is also sometimes downright difficult, when people disagree, don't get on or even get spiteful towards each other. Yet the very ordinariness, the arguments, are part of the point. Church is a place that puts you right next to your neighbour – often literally in the next seat or pew. That is the person you have to learn to love, however different they are from you, and you can't love them if you never meet them or talk to them. If they are in church, like you they presumably have some kind of faith that makes it a bit easier, but the point of learning to love your neighbour in church is that you get a bit better at loving your neighbour who doesn't share a faith, a common outlook on life or who, in fact, might not share anything much with you at all. And the point of learning to love your neighbour is that you might even start loving your enemy. If we all learnt to do that, the world would really start to change.

Most churches have their fair share of people who don't quite fit in elsewhere – those without social skills, with mental health issues or special needs. In most communities (and sometimes, let's be honest, in churches too) they are viewed as a bit of an embarrassment and you're secretly glad when they don't turn up. Yet that is a mistake.

A church that especially values the weak and the forgotten is a place of resistance to a celebrity-obsessed world, whose currency is influence, fame and power. The result of that way of life is a society in which people feel the need to prove themselves more beautiful, clever or influential than everyone else. The community of Christ, with a crucified messiah at its heart, is one that offers a radically different way – not of competition but of compassion.

Loving your enemy

If loving your neighbour is hard, try loving your enemy. Maybe you have enemies you can think of right away, maybe you don't. The word 'enemy' can cover a lot of things. It could include those who actively dislike you or make life difficult for you; it could indicate those who you would normally shun – those of a different race or religion or simply those who feel no great need to love you. Jesus' command to 'love your enemies and pray for those who persecute you'[5] is perhaps his most radical of all. And the one that seems the most unrealistic.

How do you love those who are actively hostile to you? Or merely indifferent?

The first step if I want to do this is to recognize, much as I don't like it, that God loves them as much as he loves me. When Jesus told his followers to love their enemies, he gave a reason: 'God makes his sun rise on the evil and on the good, and sends rain on the righteous and on the unrighteous.' In other words, God gives them the gift of sunshine and rain every bit as much as he does to me. It's not that being good or evil doesn't matter – it's just that, as we have seen already, there is nothing we can suffer that places us outside the love of God and nothing we can do that places us beyond the offer of the forgiveness of God.

The second step is to learn to pray for them, placing them in my mind and heart beside the God who created them (unlike me), loves them (unlike me) and sees into the real reasons why they act as they do (unlike me). When you pray for people, especially those you don't like, put them and God next to each other in your mind's eye, and you will begin to think of them not as you see them – annoying, awkward, with all kinds of obnoxious opinions – but as God sees them: precious children he created, loves and longs to see transformed into someone full of love, joy, peace and all the other things that happen in a person's heart when they open themselves to God. It's the first step towards loving people you can't stand, because there is a kind of rule of the spiritual life: it is hard to pray regularly for someone and to keep hating them.

The next step is simply to talk to them, seeing past the enmity to the person God created and loves. Bernard Shaw was once sent an invitation by a lady he didn't like much that said: 'Lady X will be at home on 23 March 1938.' He replied, writing on the back: 'Bernard Shaw will also be at home on 23 March 1938.' So often the way we express enmity is not with violence or aggression, but with avoidance. Loving our enemy means walking across the room, sending a kind email, giving a gift, establishing contact, so that at least the possibility of relationship can be opened up in which, who knows, God might change both that person's heart and mine?

The Church is a place you go to learn how to do all this – to love yourself, to love God, to love your neighbour and to love your enemy. It's a bit like the gym. A gym is a community of people who commit to a regime of discipline that will develop in them an ability to do things they otherwise couldn't. They might want to be able to play tennis, run after a bus, live a little longer or just feel healthier. So they go to health and fitness centres to do the exercises that will help them to achieve the level of fitness that lets them do all this.

In the gym, people do squats, sit-ups, bench presses and the like to develop physical health and fitness.[6] In church, people learn a different set of exercises – often called the spiritual disciplines – that develop spiritual health and fitness (or, to give it its traditional name, holiness). These are disciplines such as regular prayer, meditation, Bible reading, fasting, silence, giving, confession, celebration and the like. This 'holiness' is a quality that enables us also to do things we otherwise would not be able to do. Only this time, it is not physical activities like playing sport or running up stairs, but the ability to keep our promises even when sorely tempted not to, to be generous even when we're short of cash, to keep calm when it feels much easier to lose our temper.

Just as specific physical exercises target particular muscle groups, so particular spiritual exercises target certain qualities. Fasting (whether from food or your phone) cultivates not only the ability to pay attention to God through reminding us that we need God even more than we need food or social media, but also sympathy for the poor of the world who have no choice about going hungry. Silence teaches us contentment and self-control, rather than the constant need to chatter and be stimulated by conversation and external noise. Sacrifice – giving money or possessions away from time to time – teaches generosity so that it becomes less a momentary response to a TV appeal but more a way of life built into everyday activity. And we do all this together. We need each other to hold us accountable, to encourage each other on this path, to remind each other of the goal, to rejoice at successes or to support each other when the going is hard. There is a rule of life that we become like the people we spend time with, so we need to surround ourselves with examples of kindness, humility, love and generosity, whether that is Christians who have walked this way before (that's why many Christian churches like to remember the saints, great Christians of the past who showed us how to live in this way) or people in our local Christian community who can show us what these things look like in practice.

If you try a local church and it isn't immediately the most exciting place or if you're already trying one and its hard work because the people aren't exactly the ones you'd choose or are just a bit irritating, don't be put off. There's a passage in one of St Paul's letters where he writes to one the churches he's founded along these lines:

Therefore, as God's chosen people, holy and dearly loved, clothe yourselves with compassion, kindness, humility, gentleness and patience. Bear with each other and forgive one another if any of you has a grievance against someone. Forgive as the Lord forgave you.[7]

It's a strange list of qualities – nothing about bravery, courage, entrepreneurship or changing the world. But it's realistic. If you're going to live together with other people, even in a community that is trying to live differently, you're going to need qualities such as humility, patience and forgiveness, because there will be people who make you feel humble, people who will try your patience, people who you will need to forgive and from whom you might need to ask forgiveness. In a way that is the point. The world is truly changed for the better not by bull-in-a-china-shop mavericks, but by people who have learnt compassion, kindness, humility, gentleness and patience, and who slowly but surely change the atmosphere around them as they live.

Followers of Jesus are far from the finished product. They are just people who know both their greatness and their wretchedness, that they are a complex mix of victim and villain. Yet because God who made the world has defeated the darkness in that world and in their hearts, they have become new people. They no longer feel the need to impress, hoping a sceptical world will see their inner genius, but live instead out of the knowledge that they are loved, are never alone, always forgiven, and reorientated towards the light. They are starting to open out from the curvature of the soul that affects every one of us. So, for the rest of their days, they become part of the resistance, part of a host of small communities scattered around the world, looking forward to the day when evil will be banished and love will win. They are learning to love God and their neighbour. Everything else is detail.

What do I do now?

If you've got to the end of this book, first of all, well done. It may be that you picked it up because you were curious about the title. You may have been curious about Christianity and, even if you weren't when you started, you may want to tentatively take it a step further now. So what do you do? Here are a few ideas.

- Why not start by reading one of the Gospels – if you want a tip to get you going, try the Gospel of Mark, as it's the shortest and most action-packed.
- You might want to start trying to pray. The simplest prayer to pray is the Lord's Prayer. You can also find simple guides online – go to <www.churchofengland.org> and type in 'Learning to Pray' or 'Lord's Prayer'. You could also try <www.24-7prayer.com> and look up the section on 'Help me Pray'.
- There are lots of courses out there that can help you ask your questions about what it's like to be a Christian. The best known is the Alpha Course – alpha.org. If you check out the websites of churches near you, you'll probably find one that is running it, either online or in person. Other churches might be running something called the Pilgrim Course or Christianity Explored. They are a great way to meet new people, dip your toe in the water of church and weigh it all up over a few weeks. Just sign up, take a deep breath and take the plunge.
- The last chapter might have made you want to try a church. If so, look up <www.achurchnearyou.com> and try one that looks friendly and welcoming.

- If you want to do a bit more reading, try these:

  - Francis Spufford (2012) *Unapologetic: Why, despite everything, Christianity can still make surprising emotional sense* (London: Faber & Faber).
  - Pete Greig (2019) *How to Pray: A simple guide for normal people* (London: Hodder & Stoughton).
  - Timothy Radcliffe (2005) *What Is the Point of Being a Christian?* (London: Burns & Oates).
  - David Bentley Hart (2011) *The Doors of the Sea: Where was God in the Tsunami?* (Grand Rapids, MI: Eerdmans) – on the problem of evil.
  - Graham Tomlin (2017) *Bound to be Free: The paradox of freedom* (London: Bloomsbury) – on the meaning of freedom.

Notes

1 Why 'being yourself' is a bad idea

1 There is a proper debate about whether the world is getting better or worse. For an optimistic view, see S. Pinker (2018) *Enlightenment Now: The case for reason, science, humanism and progress* (London: Penguin Random House). For a critique of his sunny optimism, see Nick Spencer's review, available online at: <https://theosthinktank.co.uk/comment/2018/02/20/enlightenment-and-progress-or-why-steven-pinker-is-wrong>. Alternatively for, to my mind, a more realistic view, try J. Gray (1995) *Enlightenment's Wake: Politics and culture at the close of the modern age* (Abingdon: Routledge).

2 J. M. Twenge and Keith W. Campbell (2010) *The Narcissism Epidemic* (New York: Free Press). Quoted in W. Storr (2017) *Selfie: How the West became self-obsessed* (London: Picador), p. 228.

3 *Luther's Works* 25.291.

4 Storr, *Selfie*.

5 C. Taylor (1989) *Sources of the Self: The making of the modern identity* (Cambridge: Cambridge University Press) and C. Taylor (1991) *The Ethics of Authenticity* (Cambridge, MA, and London: Harvard University Press).

6 For more on this, see C. Taylor (2007) *A Secular Age* (Cambridge, MA, and London: Belknap Press).

7 If you're interested in this point, read this: P. J. Deneen (2018) *Why Liberalism Failed* (New Haven, CT: Yale University Press).

8 L. Hunt (2007) *Inventing Human Rights: A history* (New York: W. W. Norton).

9 If you're interested in this approach and want to read more of Hartmut Rosa's work, try these: (2013) *Social Acceleration: A new theory of modernity* (New York Columbia University Press); (2019)

Resonance: A sociology of our relationship to the world (Cambridge : Polity Press).

10 Mark 8.35 (MSG).

2 Why wonder is the beginning of wisdom

1 J. Barnes (1989) *A History of the World in 10½ Chapters* (London: Cape).

2 The long and slightly tortuous title of the poem is *Ode: Intimations of immortality from recollections of early childhood.*

3 L. M. Krauss (2012) *A Universe from Nothing: Why there is something rather than nothing* (London: Simon & Schuster).

4 I'm aware of the difficulties regarding which pronoun to use for God – he, she or it? God is presumably not male. Or female. But Christians believe that God is a person – and that is why 'it' doesn't work. Switching between 'he' and 'she' is clumsy and awkward. So I've gone with the traditional 'he', 'his' and so on. NOT, I stress, because God is male, but because our language has to go with one of our two personal pronouns and many years of usage has established that as the most common way. If you find it a problem, I hope you'll bear with me and understand the dilemma.

5 D. B. Hart (2013) *The Experience of God: Being, consciousness, bliss* (New Haven, CT: Yale), p. 143.

6 Acts 17.28.

7 G. K. Chesterton (1986) *Saint Thomas Aquinas, Saint Francis of Assisi* (San Francisco, CA: Ignatius Press), p. 159.

3 Why love is and isn't all you need

1 Stuart Howarth (2009) *I Just Wanted to Be Loved* (London: Harper Element).

2 C. S. Lewis (1960) *The Four Loves* (Glasgow: Collins). *The Four Loves* by C. S. Lewis copyright © CS Lewis Pte Ltd 1960. Extracts reprinted by permission.

3 Lewis, *The Four Loves*, pp. 116–17. *The Four Loves* by C. S. Lewis copyright © CS Lewis Pte Ltd 1960. Extracts reprinted by permission.

4 N. Luhmann (1986) *Love as Passion: The codification of intimacy* (Cambridge: Polity Press) and N. Luhmann (2010) *Love: A sketch* (Cambridge: Polity Press).

5 S. Kierkegaard (1962) *Works of Love* (New York: Harper Perennial).

6 Kierkegaard, *Works of Love*, p. 25.

7 Kierkegaard, *Works of Love*, p. 158.

8 Augustine (1998) *Confessions* (Oxford: Oxford University Press), p. 35.

4 Why the Big Bang has a face

1 John 4.8.

2 The same is true of the Hindu Upanishads and the Confucian Analects.

3 I'm aware this chapter assumes that the Gospels give us an account of Jesus in his context that is broadly historical, rather than a set of wild legends. I don't have time or space to establish that here, but there's a lot of evidence to suggest the authors were at least trying to write something that looks a bit like our notions of historical biography. If you're interested, see R. Bauckham (2006) *Jesus and the Eyewitnesses: The Gospels as eyewitness testimony* (Grand Rapids, MI: Eerdmans); or R. A. Burridge (2004) *What are the Gospels? A comparison with Graeco-Roman biography* (Grand Rapids, MI: Eerdmans).

4 M. O. C. Walshe (1995) *The Long Discourses of the Buddha: A translation of the Digha Nikaya* (Boston, MA: Wisdom Publications), p. 176.

5 Mark 2.7.

6 Matthew 13.41; 24.31; 25.31.

7 John 20.28–29.

8 Zechariah 9.9.

9   Colossians 1.15.

10 Hebrews 1.3.

11 John 1.18.

12 John 1.14.

13 G. K. Chesterton (1925) *The Everlasting Man* (London: Hodder & Stoughton), p. 176.

14 The four Gospels – Matthew. Mark, Luke and John – found at the beginning of the New Testament in the Bible, were composed by followers of Jesus in the decades after his time with them, relying on individual stories that circulated in the early communities of Jesus' followers and had a much stronger sense of oral transmission than we have today. That oral culture, with all kinds of checks and balances that kept an eye on aberrations from the original story, served as a brake on too much imaginative elaboration, ensuring that they give us a pretty accurate picture of Jesus in his time. See K. E. Bailey (1983) *Poet and Peasant and Through Peasant Eyes: A literary-cultural approach to the parables in Luke* (Combined Edition, Grand Rapids, MI: Eerdmans).

15 C. S. Lewis (1960) *The Four Loves* (Glasgow: Collins), p. 116. *The Four Loves* by C. S. Lewis copyright © CS Lewis Pte Ltd 1960. Extracts reprinted by permission.

16 Luke 19.1–10.

17 John 8.2–11.

18 Luke 7.11–15.

19 Hebrews 1.3.

20 Colossians 1.15.

21 Matthew 17.1–13.

22 Acts 17.23.

23 1 John 1.1–2.

24 John 3.35; 5.20.

25 2 Timothy 1.7.

26 F. Nietzsche (1996) *On the Genealogy of Morals* (Oxford: Oxford Universtiy Press), p. 21.

27 Nietzsche, *On the Genealogy of Morals*, p. 7.

28 For two recent examples of many arguments along these lines, see T. Holland (2019) *Dominion: The making of the Western mind* (London: Little, Brown); N. Spencer (2016) *The Evolution of the West: How Christianity has shaped our values* (London: SPCK).

29 Mark 12.30.

5 Why evil exists and why it can't be explained

1 F. Dostoevsky (1981) *The Brothers Karamazov* (Toronto: Bantam), pp. 295–6.

2 Genesis 1.31.

3 Afterword in L. M. Krauss (2012) *A Universe from Nothing: Why there is something rather than nothing* (London: Simon & Schuster), p. 188.

4 C. S. Lewis (2013) *The Weight of Glory: A collection of Lewis' most moving addresses* (London: Collins), p. 30. *The Weight of Glory* by C. S. Lewis copyright © CS Lewis Pte Ltd 1949. Extracts reprinted by permission.

6 Why justice matters and why we don't really want it

1 Genesis 6.6.

2 B. Pascal (1966) *Pensées* (Harmondsworth: Penguin), p. 59.

3 W. Storr (2017) *Selfie: How the West became self-obsessed* (London: Picador), p. 317.

7 Why everyone needs an identity crisis

1 Revelation 21.3–4.

2 Luke 22.53 (NIV).

3 Matthew 27.46.

4 2 Timothy 1.10 (author's paraphrase).

5 Luke 23.34.

6 Luke 24.36.

7 See at: <https://theatlantic.com/magazine/archive/2015/04/the-science-of-near-death-experiences/386231> (accessed 21 June 2020).

8 2 Corinthians 5.17 (author's paraphrase).

9 Ephesians 4.22 (NIV).

10 B. Chatwin (1987) *The Songlines* (London: Picador), p. 148.

11 Ephesians 2.10.

12 Luke 23.34.

8 Why freedom is not what you think it is

1 For a fuller treatment of the theme of this chapter, see G. Tomlin (2017) *Bound to be Free: The paradox of freedom* (London: Bloomsbury).

2 J. Locke (1988) *Two Treatises of Government* (Cambridge: Cambridge University Press), p. 284.

3 J.-J. Rousseau (2103) *Emile* (New York: Dover), p. 58.

4 W. Kessen (1978) 'Rousseau's Children', *Daedalus*, 107(3): 155–66.

5 Galatians 5.1.

9 Why praying is dangerous

1 J. Carrette and R. King (2005) *Selling Spirituality: The silent takeover of religion* (London: Routledge), p. 156.

2 J. Kabat-Zinn (1994) *Wherever You Go, There You Are: Mindfulness meditation in everyday life* (New York: Hyperion), p. 4.

3 R. Bretherton, J. Collicutt and J. Brickman (2016) *Being Mindful, Being Christian: A guide to mindful discipleship* (Oxford: Monarch), p. 19.

4 Matthew 6.25–29.

5 Matthew 6.34 (MSG).

6 Psalm 8.4.

7 G. K. Chesterton (1996) *Orthodoxy* (London: Hodder & Stoughton).

8 If you want to read more about the mysteries of prayer answered and unanswered, look at P. Greig (2007) *God on Mute: Engaging the silence of unanswered prayer* (Eastbourne: Kingsway) or for a more in-depth theological treatment, P. S. Fiddes (2000) *Participating in God: A pastoral doctrine of the Trinity* (London: Darton, Longman & Todd), Chapter 4.

9 D. Coupland (2004) *Hey Nostradamus!* (London: Harper Perennial).

10 C. S. Lewis (ed.) (1946) *George MacDonald: An anthology* (London: Bles), pp. 51–2.

11 B. Pascal (1966) *Pensées* (Harmondsworth: Penguin), p. 152.

10 Why we can't live alone

1 K. Vonnegut (1981) *Palm Sunday: An autobiographical collage* (New York: Dial Press).

2 See J. K. A. Smith (2009) *Desiring the Kingdom: Worship, worldview and cultural formation* (Grand Rapids, MI: Baker Academic) for a discussion of the ways in which shopping malls and other such spaces act like 'cultural liturgies to shape and form people in particular ways'.

3 B. Pascal (1963) *Ouvres Complètes* (Paris: Editions de Seuil), p. 519 (author's translation).

4 M. Ignatieff (1984) *The Needs of Strangers* (London: Chatto & Windus), p. 5.

5 Matthew 5.44.

6 If you find this image of church as a kind of spiritual gym helpful, I have explored it a lot further in G. Tomlin (2006) *Spiritual Fitness: Christian character in a consumer culture* (London: Continuum).

7 Colossians 3.12–13 (NIV).

WE HAVE A VISION OF A WORLD IN WHICH EVERYONE IS TRANSFORMED BY CHRISTIAN KNOWLEDGE

As well as being an award-winning publisher, SPCK is the oldest Anglican mission agency in the world.

Our mission is to lead the way in creating books and resources that help everyone to make sense of faith.

Will you partner with us to put good books into the hands of prisoners, great assemblies in front of schoolchildren and reach out to people who have not yet been touched by the Christian faith?

To donate, please visit www.spckpublishing.co.uk/donate or call our friendly fundraising team on 020 7592 3900.